I0866779

Ilan Stavans

Selected Translations, 2000–2020

Pitt Poetry Series Ed Ochester, Editor

ilan stavans
selected translations
poems 2000–2020

University of Pittsburgh Press

Published by the University of Pittsburgh Press, Pittsburgh, Pa., 15260

Manufactured in the United States of America
Printed on acid-free paper
10 9 8 7 6 5 4 3 2 1

ISBN 13: 978-0-8229-6660-9
ISBN 10: 0-8229-6660-3

Cover art: José Gurvich, *Mundo fantástico en colores puros*, 1967. Oil on wood, 120 x 161 cm.
Cover design: Joel W. Coggins

To Jules Chametzky

And Enoch walked with God and he was no more, for God took him.

Genesis 5:24

TRANSLATED BY ROBERT ALTER

Contents

Preface: Translation and Hallucination xv

Selected Translations

Delmira Agustini (Uruguay)
Fiera de amor 3

Humberto Ak'Abal (Guatemala)
The Dance 4
I Took Your Name Out of My Mind 5

Anna Akhmatova (Russia)
The Muse 6

Yehuda Amichai (Israel)
The Diameter of the Bomb 7

Enriqueta Arévalo Larriva (Venezuela)
We Were Not the Whole Tree 8

Yitzkhok Berliner (Poland)
Popocatépetl 9

Alberto Blanco (Mexico)
My Tribe 11
Maps 13

Jorge Luis Borges (Argentina)
Borges and I 17

Julia de Burgos (Puerto Rico)
To Julia de Burgos 18

María Calcaño (Venezuela)
Cosmos 20

Paul Celan (Germany)
Death Fugue 21

Luis Alberto Crespo (Venezuela)
Hurts 23
He Who I See in My Eyes Seeing Me 24

Rubén Darío (Nicaragua)
Lo fatal 25

Carlos Drummond de Andrade (Brazil)
International Congress of Fear 26

Federico García Lorca (Spain)
At a Young Woman's Ear 27
Ode to Walt Whitman 28

Juan Gelman (Argentina)
End 33
Epitaph 34
Dibaxu: I 35
Dibaxu: XII 36

Jacqueline Goldberg (Venezuela)
Poetics 37

Ida Gramcko (Venezuela)
Jewish Cemetery (Prague) (fragment) 38
Snail, Brother 39

León de Grieff (Colombia)
White Moon 40

Ferreira Gullar (Brazil)
Translating Oneself 41
Two Plus Two Is Four 42
Song to Avoid Death 43

Óscar Hahn (Chile)
Nude Descending a Staircase 44
In the Region of Water and Fire 45

Yehuda Halevi (Spain)
My Heart Is in the East 46

José Hernández (Argentina)
The Gaucho Martín Fierro, Part One, Canto 1, 1–19 47

Vicente Huidobro (Chile)
Globe-Trotter 49

Sor Juana Inés de La Cruz (Mexico)
Misguided Men 51
Stay, Shadow 54

Darío Jamarillo Agudelo (Colombia)
Love Poem 8 55
Vengeance 56

Besik Kharanauli (Georgia)
We Should Dig Out Potatoes 57

Juan Liscano (Venezuela)
Body of Love 64

Dulce María Loynáz (Cuba)
The Mirror 65
Love Is . . . 67
I Dream of Classifying . . . 68

Leopoldo Lugones (Argentina)
History of My Death 69

Juan Carlos Marset (Spain)
Embraceable 70

José Martí (Cuba)
Two Homelands 71

Kadya Molodowsky (Belarus)
God of Mercy 72

Eugenio Montejo (Venezuela)
Earthliness 74
Ithaca 75

Álvaro Mutis (Colombia)
Lament for the Death of Marcel Proust 77

Pablo Neruda (Chile)
Your Laughter 79
The Son 81
Ode to Age 83
Ode to the Andean Cordillera 85
Ode to Ángel Cruchaga 89
Ode to the Apple 92
Ode to the Flowers of Datitla 94
Ode to the Dictionary 98
Ode to Gratitude 101
Ode to Guatemala 103
Ode to the Inconsequential Day 110
Ode to Jean Arthur Rimbaud 113
Ode to the Month of August 118
Ode to the Moon 121
Ode to the Murmur 126
Ode to the Names of Venezuela 130
Ode to Night 133
Ode to Simplicity 136
Ode to Things 140
Ode to the Watermelon 144

Andrés Neuman (Argentina / Spain)
Genesis, COVID-19 147

Antonia Palacios (Venezuela)
The Obscure Animal of Dream 149
Writings of Eviction 150

João Pinto Delgado (Portugal)
Leaving Egypt 151

Gonzalo Rojas (Chile)
André Breton Turns a Hundred and Is Fine 152

Elizabeth Schön (Venezuela)
From the Ancient Laborer I 153
Lightning from the Stable 155

Alfonsina Storni (Switzerland)
Squares and Angles 156
Very Little Man 157

José Antonio Ramos Sucre (Venezuela)
Prelude 158

Guillermo Sucre (Venezuela)
I Write with Words that Have Shadow but Don't Shelter 159

Avrum Sutzkever (Belarus)
Under Your White Stars 160

Jorge Teiller (Chile)
A Poet of the Countryside 161

Ana Enriqueta Terán (Venezuela)
Stone of Speech 162
Outrageous Proof 163

César Vallejo (Peru)
Mass 164

Blanca Varela (Peru)
Curriculum Vitae 165

Raúl Zurita (Chile)
Heaven Reject 166
These are the last moments 167
1973 168
1974 169
1980 170

Appendix: Otra Vez and Más o Menos

Emily Dickinson
Poema 239 173
Poema 288 173
Poema 441 173
Poema 917 174
Poema 1017 174
Poema 1354 174

Robert Frost
Muro que separa 175

Elizabeth Bishop
Un arte 177

Richard Wilbur
La prueba 178

Walt Whitman
América 179

William Shakespeare
Ser, or not to ser 180

Acknowledgements 181

Index of Languages 183

Index of First Lines and Titles 187

Preface Translation and Hallucination

Translation is liberation. Words caught in a single language jump out, becoming worlds in another. This is all the more noticeable in poetry, where each sound, each cadence is strategically placed.

I approach translation as hallucination. I let myself go as much as possible, attuned to every type of stimulation, happy to wander as I wonder, eventually coming to the realization that the universe I am in actually depends on *me* to perpetuate itself. Throughout the process, my mind isn't fully mine. The fact that I emerge in one piece at the end is nothing short of miraculous.

I'm an immigrant. This is my condition. Immigration is untenable without translation. Translation fosters a kind of immigration. To translate is to survive on a day-to-day basis.

I started my life in Yiddish and Spanish interchangeably, then changed to Hebrew, hoping for redemption, and eventually settled in English, with other companions like Ladino saving me along the way. I am ambivalent about the term "mother tongue" to describe my first language, for where are all subsequent ones left? Are they stepmothers? Mistresses? I also don't like describing them as "firsts" because it gives them an unsustainable location. Whatever tongue one is using at the moment is first. For those reasons, I prefer a leveling of fields: all languages—all *my* languages, for that matter—are equal; I love them just the same. All are engaged in giving birth to reality.

For me it is harder to think that I was born in Mexico than to say that I was born into Yiddish and Spanish. Languages are more than a lexicon; they contain the DNA of entire civilizations. The words we use aren't really ours; we borrow them, using them to communicate not only with our contemporaries but with those who preceded us and those who will follow us. It is our responsibility to safeguard them while we also push them onto new heights. And, obviously, while creating new words, for no living language is static.

As for poetry, I disliked it when I was young; I found it remote, pedantic. Age humbles us; it was I, of course, who was being snobbish. Poetry is tradition. In the short time we have on earth, it is up to us to unpack and extend it, to become full-fledged members of that tradition.

In short, I live in translation *without an original*. Yet originals are sacred to me, starting with the Bible. My duty as translator is to inject them with energy, to make them urgent.

I translate not only from languages I know—if it is at all possible to say that one knows a language—but from those I don't know. My heroes are John Florio, who made Montaigne feel comfortable in English and, on the way, defined Shakespeare; Richard Burton, whose *One Thousand and One Nights* is exquisite; Samuel Beckett, who rendered Sor Juana Inés de la Cruz and other colonial Mexican poets in Spanish without knowing a word of it; Joseph Brodsky, who wrote in English while anchored in Russian and vice versa; Jorge Luis Borges, who in 1943, in an essay on William Beckford's *Vathek*, argued that "the original is unfaithful to the translation"; and Adrienne Rich, who appreciated, perhaps disingenuously, that if language is power, silence is violence.

This volume features about a hundred translations done over two decades. They were carried out sporadically at the request of a friend or editor. I at times translate bi-directionally: the appendix includes sample translations into Spanish and Spanglish of poems by Elizabeth Bishop, Emily Dickinson, Robert Frost, William Shakespeare, Richard Wilbur, and Walt Whitman.

Robert Frost was dead wrong in saying that poetry is what is lost in translation. It is the other way around: poetry is born out of it.

Ilan Stavans Selected Translations, 2000–2020

Delmira Agustini

URUGUAY, 1886–1914

Fiera de amor

Spanish

Beast of love, I suffer hunger for hearts.
Of pigeons, vultures, roe deer, or lions,
There is no more tempting prey, no more gratifying tastes,
It already strangulated my claws and instinct,
When erected in an almost ethereal plinth,
I was fascinated by a statue of antique emperor.

And I grew in enthusiasm; through the stone stem
My desire ascended like fulminous ivy,
Up to the chest, seemingly nurtured in snow;
And I clamored to the impossible heart . . . the statue,
A custodian of its glory, pure and serene,
With its forehead in Tomorrow and its feet in Yesterday.

My perennial desire, the stone stem
Has been suspended like bloody ivy;
And since then I bite my heart while dreaming
Of the statue, supreme prisoner of my beautiful claw;
It is neither flesh nor marble; a star paste
Bloodless, with neither warmth nor palpitation . . .

With the essence of a superhuman passion!

Humberto Ak'Abal

GUATEMALA, 1952–2019

The Dance

K'iche'

All of us dance
on the edge of a coin.

The poor—because they are poor—
lose their step,
and fall

and everyone else
falls on top.

I Took Your Name Out from My Mind

Spanish

I took your name out of my mind
and lost it in the mountain.

It was picked up by the air
and found its path
through the ravine.

Suddenly
it crashed against the cliffs
and bounced back:

rain made it sing
and your name reached me while crying.

Anna Akhmatova

RUSSIA, 1889–1966

The Muse

Russian

At night, as I await her arrival,
my life comes to an impasse. And, truly,
what are honors, youth, or liberty
before a cherished friend with a flute!
There she is, making an entrance. She unveils herself
and looks me over at length.
I say: "Is it you who dictated to Dante
the pages of Hell?" And she answers: "It's me."

Yehuda Amichai

ISRAEL, 1924–2000

The Diameter of the Bomb

Hebrew

The diameter of the bomb was thirty centimeters
and, with four dead and eleven wounded,
the diameter of its actual range about seven meters.
And around these, in an expanding circle
of pain and time, two hospitals are scattered
and one graveyard. But the young woman
buried in the city she came from,
at a distance of more than a hundred kilometers,
expands the circle substantially,
and the lonely man mourning her death
at the far-away shores of a country across the sea
includes the whole world in the circle.
And I won't mention the howl of orphans
reaching up to God's throne and
beyond, making
a circle with no end and no God.

Enriqueta Arevalo Larriva

VENEZUELA, 1886–1962

We Were Not the Whole Tree

Spanish

We were not the whole tree. Only graceful
branches, moss-covered bark, humid flowers,
roots liberated from the abyss.

We were not always the tree.
We didn't weather frosted, stubborn rain
or keep vigil in a night of ghosts.

And we were delightedly sheltered
in its own hollow, not its hollow.

If they burned the summer frowns,
with laughter we jumped into the well.

If ax arms were lifted,
woodcutting ballads would beat us.

If fire lines advanced,
rower and horse rhymed our fugue.

If devouring ants climbed,
we were only a mirror of disaster.

If the afternoon dragged it by shadows,
we would go to the heart of the west
to play with the sun, cooled and red.

And when the wind threatened like a giant,
foreboding the uncongealing, we saved ourselves.

We were not the whole tree.
We were not always the tree.
But the miracle fully perpetuates:
My branches are nurtured by your impulse,
my uneasiness evaporates in your resin.

Yitzkhok Berliner

POLAND, 1878–1950

Popocatépetl

Yiddish

Popo—
lying stolid with a plumage of stone,
crying from your body, with a quiet scream,
are thousands of years.

in the bluish dawn of rose,
the sun hides its whitish head
with rainbow stripes,
like a hairband.

Winds—
hidden monsters in the gallop,
throwing themselves onto you, yelling as they pillage,
humming songs and whistling
from unknown lands.

what secrets,
stored in the passing of generations,
are hidden inside you?

what scars
stapled in blood,
are engraved in individual stones?

Carry me inside your body, Popo,
stone-like,
conveying
your mysteries in my silence.

Popo—
furtive hoary giant,
the sun throws you a ray
in the darkening moments of dusk,
enlightening you fully.

I see in you now
ancient generations gone,
their blood spilled
from your vertebral column.

What plethora of travelers wandered on your silvery skin?
Have you counted their steps?

At your knees
death announces its journey,
and on your back,
this frigid, whitish
pours inscrutability . . .

Alberto Blanco

MEXICO, 1951–

My Tribe

Spanish

The earth is the same
    the heavens are different.
The heavens are the same
    the earth is different.

From lake to lake,
from one forest to another:
which is my tribe?
—I ask—
which is my place?

Perhaps I belong to the tribe
of them with none;
or the tribe of black sheep;
or a tribe whose ancestors
    emerge from the future:
a tribe yet to come.

But if I am to belong to a tribe
—I tell myself—
let it be a large tribe,
a strong tribe,
a tribe where nothing and no one
is left outside,
where everyone,
everything and always
have a holy place.

I don't mean a human tribe.
I don't mean a planetary tribe.
I don't even mean a universal tribe.
I mean a tribe about which one cannot speak.

I mean a tribe that forever lived
but whose existence is yet to be proven.

A tribe that has never lived
but whose existence
might now be proven.

Maps

Spanish

I

Let's start at the beginning:
Earth is not the earth:
The map is not the territory.
The territory is not the map.

A map is an image.
A map is a way of speaking.
A map is a collection of memories.
A map is a proportional representation.

The four winds, four rivers, four doors, four pillars of the earth of which myths talk about are nothing but the four corners of a map.

Every map is an image, a painting, a metaphor, a description . . .
But not every description, metaphor, image, or, given the case, not every painting is—by necessity—a map.
Although it can become one.

II

A map is nothing—as the *Nabi* painter Maurice Denis said of all paintings—but an arrangement of forms and colors over a bi-dimensional surface.

If a territory were homogenous, only the profile of the limits of the territory would be accounted in a map.

No trees grow in a map.

A map of the real world is no less imaginary than a map of an imaginary world.

III

A map is nothing but a bi-dimensional representation of a tri-dimensional world visited by a ghost: time.

If we have been able to map a three-dimensional world in two dimensions, it ought to be possible to map a four-dimensional world in three dimensions.

With a holographic map time should be able to be mapped.

Just like the earth does not stop changing with time, the history of maps does not stop changing with history.
Our idea of space changes according to the changes of our idea of time.

IV

Every map begins with a journey.
But, does every journey start with a map?

The map is to a journey what myth is to language.

At the beginning, maps were travel stories.
Later maps were sights at the edge of the horizon: visual narratives.
Finally, seen from a bird's eye: geographical poems.

A map is an artistic manifestation of the fear of the unknown.

V

To look at the earth from above: arrogance of a fake god.

At the beginning the maps of the earth were accompanied by the maps of heaven.
Later on maps were left without a heaven.
If things go on like this, very soon maps will be left without an earth.

Any truth that can be told is no truth.
Words are not what they designate.
Maps of the earth are not the earth.
The stellar charts are not the heavens.

A dot is a town.
A line is a freeway.
A colored surface is a country.
A volume must be the map of a history.

VI

Exterior maps: Geography.
Interior maps: Psychology.
The doors are the senses.
The limits are the body.

The moral to be drawn from the maps has to do with the idea of control, or—in the best of cases—with an idea of conservation.

As one thinks of the direct relation that exists between maps, the earnings, the wars of conquest and the control of time, one cannot but think of the poem's title:
"A Chronometer and Artillery Map."

A map the size of a man's ambition.
A man's ambition the size of a referential system.

All points of reference in a map look outward.

VII

Maps are ideal portraits of our mother.

Maps look at us face to face when they showcase their surfaces.
When they want to account for their depth, they look at us sideways.

At the beginning of cartography it was not possible—perhaps not even desirable—to separate the territories of wakefulness from the landscapes of dream.

What are the colors on a map if not a dream?
The anesthetized memory of our childhood.
The open windows in the cartographer's office.
A fountain of the purest, simplest happiness.

VIII

Every map is an island.

What once was a savage territory is now a map.

All writing is fragmentary.
Every map is fragmentary.

On maps no travel ever takes place.
In poetry there's nothing written.

Jorge Luis Borges

ARGENTINA, 1899–1986

Borges and I

Spanish

The other one, Borges, is to whom things happen. I walk through Buenos Aires, stop, maybe a bit mechanically, to look at the arch of an entrance way and a grillwork door; I have news from Borges by mail or when I see his name on a list of professors or in a biographical dictionary. I like hourglasses, maps, 18th-century typography, the taste of coffee, and Stevenson's prose; the other shares those preferences but with a vanity that turns them into an actor's attributes. It would be an exaggeration to affirm that our relationship is hostile; I live, I let myself live, so that Borges can plot his literature, and that literature justifies me. It doesn't cost me anything to confess he has achieved a few valid pages, but those pages can't save me, perhaps because what's good no longer belongs to anyone, not even to the other, but to language and tradition. In any case, I'm destined to be lost, definitively, and just some instant of me will survive in the other. Little by little I cede everything, even though I'm aware of his perverse tendency to falsify and pontificate. Spinoza understood that all things want to be preserved in their being: the stone eternally wants to be a stone and the tiger a tiger. I shall remain in Borges, not in myself (if I am someone), but I recognize myself less in his books than in many by others and in the laborious strumming of a guitar. Years ago I tried freeing myself from him and went from the mythologies of the arrabal to the games with time and the infinite, but those games are Borges' now and I shall come up with other things. Thus my life is a flight and I lose everything and everything belongs to oblivion, or to the other.

I don't know which of the two writes this page.

Julia de Burgos

PUERTO RICO, 1917–1953

To Julia de Burgos

Spanish

Already people murmur I'm your enemy
since they say that in verse I give the world to me.

They lie, Julia de Buros. They lie, Julia de Burgos.
The one rising in my verses isn't your voice: it is my voice
since you are costumes and I, the essence; and the
deepest abyss spreads between us.

You are the cold doll of a social lie,
and I the virile flash of human truth.

You, honey of courtesan hypocrisy; not me;
in all my poems I undress the heart.

You are like your world, selfish;
not me; I gamble everything to be who I am.

You are only the severe ladylike señorona; not me;
I am life, strength, woman.

You are of your husband, of your master; not me;
I am nobody's, or everyone's, since I give myself to everyone,
to everyone in my pure feeling and in my thought.

You curl your hair and wear makeup; not me;
the wind curls me, the sun is my makeup.

You are a house dame, resigned, submissive,
tied up in male prejudice; not me;
I am Rocinante breaking out in gallop
snorting God's landscapes in search of justice.

You don't rule yourself;
everyone rules you; your husband rules you, your
parents, your relatives, the priest, the tailor,

the theater, casino, and car,
jewels, banquet, champagne, sky
and hell, and the what-will-they-say.

Not me; only my heart rules,
my thought; I rule myself.

You, aristocratic flower; and I, people's flower.
You have everything in you and you owe it
to everyone, whereas I don't owe a thing to anyone.

You, nailed to the unmovable ancestral dividend,
and I, a one in in social accountant's tally
we are the deadly duel that fatefully approaches.

When the masses riot without stop
leaving behind in ashes the burnt injustices.
and when, with the torch of seven virtues
it pursues the seven sins, the masses run away,
against you, and against what is unjust and inhuman
it will be me in their midst with the torch in hand.

María Calcaño

VENEZUELA, 1906–1956

Cosmos

Spanish

A grand nakedness
my body
and the night . . .

But I dream of dawn!

Dawn:
opening of blood
and wings.

And the bird
owner of the forest
with a trill . . .

Life
is a pile of fertile soil!

Man
and I
are the chimera.

God
in his grave truth!

And above us
like a curse
that monstrous shadow . . .

Paul Celan

GERMANY, 1920–1970

Death Fugue

German

Black milk in the morning we drink you at dawn
we drink you at noon in the morning we drink you at night
we drink you and drink you
we dig the grave in heaven it is wide to lie there
A man in the house he toys with the serpents and he writes
he writes to Deutschland at dusk your golden
    hair Margarete
he writes it down and walks away from the house the stars scintillate he
    whistles for his dog to come
he whistles for his Jews and orders a grave to
    be dogged in the soil
he orders us to perform the dance

Black milk in the morning we drink you at dawn
we drink you at noon in the morning we drink you at night
we drink you and drink you
A man in the house he toys with the serpents and he writes
he writes to Deutschland at dusk your golden
    hair Margarete
Your ashen hair Shulamit we dig a grave in
    heaven it is
wide to lie there

He shrieks jab it deep in the soil you there and you others
    sing and perform
he holds the metal in his belt and swings and his eyes
    are blue
jab deeper your metal there and you others perform
    again the dance

Black milk in the morning we drink you at dawn
we drink you at noon in the morning we drink you at night
we drink you and drink you
a man in the house your golden hair Margarete
your ashen hair Shulamit he toys with the serpents

He screams perform the music of sweet death commands as a
master for Deutschland
he shrieks play the fiddle more somber like smoke
you will climb to heaven
then dig a grave for you in the clouds it is wide to lie
to lie there

Black milk in the morning we drink you at dawn
we drink you at noon death arrives as a command from
Deutschland
we drink you at dusk and dawn we drink you and
drink you
a master for Deutschland and his eyes are
blue
with a lead bullet he will reach his target he will reach
you
a man in the house your golden hair Margarete
he pursues us with dogs in heaven he digs us a
grave
he performs with the serpents and dreams that death arrives as
a command for Deutschland

your golden hair Margarete
your ashen hair Shulamit

Luis Alberto Crespo

VENEZUELA, 1941–

Hurts

Spanish

The crack without a house
when I'm not found

The injury of the knocker
striking me where I'm still absent

That hurts
to live far without hearing from myself

the body inside, listening, still

He Who I See in My Eyes Seeing Me

Spanish

Bird without leaves

Its fixed flight
The sole sheet

I catch its height in the erosion

It selects me
To complain

My surrender is its scream

Rubén Darío

NICARAGUA, 1867–1916

Lo fatal

Spanish

to René Pérez

The tree is happy for it's barely sentient,
and the hard rock more so for it feels nothing.
There's no greater pain than being alive,
no bigger despair than conscious life.

To be and not to know, to be without a path,
the dread of having been and a terror to come . . .
The sure freight of being dead tomorrow,
to suffer for life, through darkness, and for

that which we know not and barely suspect,
the tempting flesh, its grape bunch to come,
the tomb that awaits with its funeral sprays,
not to know where we go,
nor where we came from . . . !

Carlos Drummond de Andrade

BRAZIL, 1902–1987

International Congress of Fear

Portuguese

Provisionally we shall not sing to love,
which hides far below the underground.
We shall sing to fear, sterilizing embraces,
we shall not sing to hatred, which exists barely,
fear barely exists, our father and companion,
the great fear of heartlands, of seas, of deserts
the fear of soldiers, the fear of mothers, the fear of churches,
we shall sing to the fear of dictators, the fear of democrats,
we shall sing to the fear of death and the fear of after death.
Then we will die of fear
and over our graves yellow, fearful flowers will rise.

Federico García Lorca

SPAIN, 1898–1936

At a Young Woman's Ear

Spanish

I didn't want to.
I didn't want to say anything.
I saw in your eyes
two crazy trees
of breeze, laughter, and gold.
They moved.
I didn't want to.

Ode to Walt Whitman

Spanish

Along the East River and the Bronx
the young men were singing baring their waists,
with the wheel, the oil, the leather and the hammer.
Ninety thousand miners dug up silver from the rocks
and the children drew staircases and perspectives.

But none slept,
none wanted to be the river,
none loved the big leaves,
none the blue lagoon on the beach.

Along the East River and Queensborough
the young fought the industry,
and the Jews sold to the fawn in the river
the rose of circumcision
and the sky flowed along the bridges and the roofs
herds of bison pushed by the wind.

But none stopped,
none wanted to be cloud,
none searched for the fern
or the small drum's yellow wheel.

When the moon appears
the pulleys will roll to bring down the sky;
an edge of needles will fence in memory
and coffins will take away those who don't work.

New York of silt,
New York of wire and death.
What angel do you hide in your cheek?
What perfect voice shall say truths of wheat?
Who the terrible dream of its tainted anemone?

Not a single moment, old beautiful Walt Whitman,
have I stopped seeing your beard full of butterflies,
or your velveteen shoulders consumed by the moon,
or your tights of virginal Apollo,
or your voice like a column of ash;
beautiful old man like fog
who moaned like a bird
with their sex crossed by a needle,
enemy of satyr,
enemy of vine,
and lover of bodies under the plain cloth.
Not a single moment, virile beauty
who in hills of carbon, ads and trains,
dreamed of being a river and sleeping like a river
with that comrade who would put on your chest
a little pain of ignorant leopard.

Not a single moment, Adam of blood, macho,
man alone at sea, old beautiful Walt Whitman,
because along the terrace roofs,
gathered in bars,
emerging in clusters from the sewers,
trembling on the legs of chauffeurs
or rotating in the platforms of wormwood,
queers, Walt Whitman, dreamed you.

That one also! Also! And they descend
on your luminous beard and caste,
blonds of the north, black from the sand,
multitudes screaming and gesticulating,
like cats and like serpents,
queers, Walt Whitman, queers
muddy with tears, meat for riding crop,
boot and tamer's bite.

That one also! Also! Fingers dyed
signal the edge of your dream
when the friend eats an apple
with a slight taste of gasoline
and the sun sings along the navels
of young men playing under the bridges.

But you didn't look for scratched eyes,
or the darkest swamp where the children are submerged,
or the frozen saliva,
or wounded curves like a toad's belly
that queers are carrying in cars and roofs
while the moon beats them along the corners of terror.

You were looking for bareness like a river,
bull and dream that joints the wheel with the algae,
father of your agony, camellia of your death,
and moaning in the flames of your hidden equator.

Because it is fair for man no to look for his pleasure
In the jungle of blood of the nearby morning.
The sky had beaches to evade life
and bodies not to be repeated at dawn.

Agony, agony, dream, ferment and dream.
This is the world, friend, agony, agony.
The dead decompose under the clock of the cities,
war passes by crying with a million gray rats,
the rich giving away their lovers
small illuminated dying men,
and life isn't noble, good, or sacred.

Man can, if ready, tame his desire
along the coral vein or blue nakedness.

Tomorrow the loves will be rocks and Time
a breeze arriving asleep through the branches.

That's why I don't raise my voice, old Walt Whitman,
against the child who writes
a girl's name in his pillow,
or against the man dressed up like a bride
in the closet darkness,
or against lonely people in casinos
who drink with disgust the water of prostitution,
or against the men of green sight
who love the man and burn their lips in silence.
But I do against you, gays of the city,
of tumescent flesh and filthy thought,
mothers of mud, shrews, enemies without sleep
of Love giving away crowns of joy.

Against you always, who give to young men
drops of dirty death with sour poison.
Against you always,
Faeries of North America,
Pájaros of Habana,
Jotos of Mexico,
Sarasas of Cádiz,
Ápios of Seville,
Cancos of Madrid,
Floras of Alicante,
Adelaidas of Portugal.

Queers of the entire world, killers of doves!
slaves of woman, sluts of their dressers,
open in the plazas with fever of fan
or ambushes of rigid landscapes of hemlock.

There is no refuge! Death
emanates from your eyes
and collects gray flowers in the edge of silt.
There is no refuge! Beware!
Let the disoriented, the pure,
the classic, the signaled, the supplicant
close the door of orgy.

And you, beautiful Walt Whitman, sleep on the shores of the Hudson
with the beard toward dust and open hands.
Tender clay or snow, your tongue is calling
the comrades to keep vigil to your bodiless gazelle.
Sleep, nothing is left.
A dance of walls unsettles the prairie
and America is flooded with machines and cry.
I want the strong wind of the deepest night
to erase flowers and letters from the arch where you sleep
and a black child to announce to the white people of gold
the arrival of the kingdom of spike.

Juan Gelman

ARGENTINA, 1930–2014

End

Spanish

Poetry isn't a bird.
And is.
It isn't a lung, air, my shirt,
no, nothing like that. And all of it.
Yes.
I have broken a violet against the sunset
to see what happened,
I went to the stone and asked what happened.
But no. But no.
Not yet.
Did I perhaps forget that handkerchief
on which an old waltz circles in silence?
I didn't forget it, look at my cheek
and you'll see, no, I didn't forget it.
Did I forget the wooden horse?
Touch in me the child and you'll say no.
And so what?
Poetry is a way of living.
Look at the people at your side.
Do they eat? Suffer? Sing? Cry?

Help them fight for their hands, their eyes, their mouth, for the kiss to kiss and the kiss to give away, for their table, their bread, their letter a and their letter h, for their past—were they not children?—for their present, for the piece of peace, of history and happiness that belongs to them, for the piece of love, big, small, sad, joy, that belongs to them and is taken away in the name of what, of what?

Your life will then be an innumerable river to be called pedro, juan, ana, maría, bird, lung, the air, my shirt, violin, sunset, stone, that handkerchief, old waltz, wooden horse.

Poetry is this.
Afterward, write it.

Epitaph

Spanish

A bird lived in me.
A flower traveled in my blood.
My heart was a violin.

I loved and didn't. But sometimes
was loved. I also
was happy: about the spring,
the hands together, what is happy.

I say a man has to be!

(Herein lies a bird.
A flower.
A violin.)

Dibaxu: I

Ladino

the tremor on my lips/
I mean: the tremor of my kisses
will be heard in your past
with me in your wine/

opening the door of time/
your dream
allows sleeping rain to fall/
give me your rain/

I will stop you/ still
in your rain of sleep/
far inside the thinking/
without fear/ without forgetfulness/

in the house of time
is the past/
under your foot/
dancing/

Dibaxu: XII

Ladino

what you gave me
is the trembling word
in the hand of time
open for drinking/

silent
the house is
where we kissed
inside the sun/

Jacqueline Goldberg

VENEZUELA, 1966–

Poetics

Spanish

Suddenly the poet's mouth is overwhelmed by larvae,
such is the lightness.

One must extract them one by one
for the poem to return to its cause,
for the maelstrom of wounds to acquiesce.

The stabbed shrieks have been too many,
and also the persistence of funeral rites.

The forehead kisses the ground.
Happiness is no longer a daily affiliation.

Once the last fortune is rooted out,
the poem will need to be cut down to size,
like teeth, in a voracious trance.

The poem will grow from its own forgiveness,
offering cruxes, efforts, voyages. Leveled by a certain slavery.

And pain?
Will it need to be recovered so a book can grow within the book?
For the gash of a future tear?

To write, once more, is to exist in gloom, in the preterit,
abundant to the end.

Ida Gramcko

VENEZUELA, 1924–1994

Jewish Cemetery (Prague) (fragment)

Spanish

Order suffers, what is racked with pain ends,
everything is in white, in maidenhood, suspended,
everything is like a bird in gestation, its wings
not yet surrendered to the drunkenness of wind.
Around the virginal impatience awaiting
a bed has been growing
born from residue working
with shreds of ambit and body.
Threatened manifest destiny,
arrow shot from remains.
The self, in vertical fall, points
to a new path amidst its straight bit.
Like a face untouched
would arrive with dawn.

The new cradle's a tombstone discovered
rocking a maternal lullaby, terrain,
primal, subterranean maternity
laboring its fruit in the boiling of bones,
a cautious, tutelary mother deceiving
while covering the garden with a desert
of individual life that later rescues
from man his sepulcher, his spectrum.
Deep mother that changes names
and touches a hairdresser,
and says rain when it spots a tear
and calls rose what was a brain.
When I say: lack,
she says: heritage.
If a man kisses vanishing faces,
in kissing he finds the personal, the dead,
but she evades faces like masks
getting ready for the eternal kiss,
the one linking clot and sap
in primitive and warm concert.

Snail, Brother

Spanish

Snail, brother
the same self, but snail. Its concise form
follows with neither varnish nor ravage
for man to suffer a rich soul,
his own soul in fleece and bunch,
intimate, immense, always thirsty and satiated.
This is how we build a human site,
but as full with it as with a breeze.
We invent
a wall made of whitewash . . . And so unique!
A new wall, strange?
Alone in its fresh and continuous solitude.
"Solitude, once again that which is lonesome,
once again the distance? And tenderness?"—
Calm down, love; what is ours is distant,
it touches the long profile, the flat stone
saying through its vigorous voice; I love you.
The singular form is the infinite one.

León de Grieff

COLOMBIA, 1895–1976

White Moon

Spanish

White moon . . . and cold . . .
and my sweet heart in bold
secluded . . . secluded . . .

Your hand, eluded!

White moon, and cold
my sweet heart in bold
secluded . . .

The vague piano notes . . .
From the forest an arcane aroma . . .
And a river, resounded . . .

My sweet heart in bold,
secluded . . . !

Ferreira Gullar

BRAZIL, 1930–2016

Translating Oneself

Portuguese

A part of me
is everyone;
another part, no one:
a bottomless bottom.

A part of me
is multitude:
Another part, strangeness
and solitude.

A part of me
ponders, examines:
Another part
is delirious.

A part of me
gets lunch and dinner:
Another part
gets scared.

A part of me
is permanent:
another part
knows it's sudden.

A part of me,
is total vertigo:
another part,
language.

Translating one part
into another
—being a matter
of life and death—
is it art?

COTRANSLATED WITH TAL GOLDFAJN

Two Plus Two Is Four

Portuguese

Just as two and two is four
I know life is worth the pain
Though the bread is precious
And the freedom rare

Just as your eyes are clear
And your skin, dark

Just as the ocean is blue
And the lake, serene

Just as a time of joy
Beckons me behind the terror

And the night carries the day
In its lap of lily

—I know that two and two are four
I know that life is worth the pain

Even though the bread is precious
And the freedom, rare.

COTRANSLATED WITH TAL GOLDFAJN

Song to Avoid Death

Portuguese

When you go away
girl as white as snow,
take me with you.

If perhaps you cannot
take me by the hand,
girls white as snow,
take me to heart.

If in the heart you cannot
by chance take me,
girl of dream and snow,
take me into your memory.

And if you cannot,
for as much as it takes,
already alive in your thoughts,
girl as white as snow,
take me into oblivion.

COTRANSLATED WITH TAL GOLDFAJN

Óscar Hahn

CHILE, 1938–

Nude Descending a Staircase

Spanish

Herein the suit
the soul covers
its shame with
the suit
that one day becomes
dust
    shadow
        void

leaving the soul in open air
with no hands to cover
its private parts
Hence in some closet somewhere
in some hanger hangs the soul
        in its
            saddest
                nakedness

In the Region of Water and Fire

Spanish

Flames swimming in living water
Water swimming amid flames

Liquid color and incandescent cold

Man lives surrounded by opposites
unfriendly concepts that become one:

spiritual water and physical fire
immaterial fire and stone-like water
watery fire and flaming rivers

Wood crackles fire listens
The spring makes noise over the stones
Water falls and listens to itself

Water sleeps in fire's arms
Fire rocks the water's cradle

Water and fire: the original couple
from which being flows

As life and death are being uttered
As man and woman are being named

Yehuda Halevi

SPAIN, 1075–1141

My Heart Is in the East

Hebrew

My heart is in the east, and I am in the far-away west.
How can I savor food? How might it be sweet to me?
How might I render my vows and bonds, while
Zion in under the might of Edom and I am in Arab bondage?
It would be good for me to leave behind all goods from Spain
while I behold in my eyes the precious dust of the forsaken sanctuary.

José Hernández

ARGENTINA, 1834–1886

The Gaucho Martín Fierro, Part One, Canto 1, 1–19

Spanish

1. What I'm about to tell you is a rare tale of uncommon sorrow and I cain't do it lest I strum on my guitar. I'm like a lonely bird singing hisself to sleep.

2. And I need all the saints in heaven to do this, to hep me along, right here, right now, while I sing my song and I'm askin' all the saints to refresh my memory and clear up my thoughts. Here goes:

3. "Come, all ye miraculous saints! Come hep me now! I'm tongue-tied. I'm buggy-eyed. And God hep me, it's a rough start. Figger I'll sing my song while strummin' my guitar. It's a rare tale of uncommon sorrow."

4. I've seen lots of famous poets who after they got to be famous don't want to keep famous. I guess they got tired of it, bit by bit.

5. But that ain't what happened to Martin Fierro, no sirree. No one outdid him. No body backed him down. And even though lots of folks have already sung about him, I'm gonna sing about him anyway.

6. I'm gonna die singing. They'll bury me singing. And when I get to the feet of the Heavenly Padre, I'll still be singing. I was born to sing.

7. So let's untie my tongue, and let words not fail me. Singing will be my glory and when I set myself to singing the earth can open up and still I'll be singing.

8. I'm settin' here on this bottom land to lay out my case. Like the howling wind I'll make the prairie grass tremble. I'll wager my gold coins, drinks, bullets.

9. I got no book-learnin' but when I start to sing there's no stoppin' me. I'll die singing! Verses shoot from me like water from a gusher.

10. When I grab my guitar, not even flies land on me, nobody lays a finger on me. When my chest begins to roar, my e-string moans and my a-string weeps.

11. I'm a bull in my own rodeo and a bull-and-a-half in someone else's. I think I'm purty good and if you want to try me, you come out and sing and we'll see who's worse.

12. No flick-knife backs me down, let the cut-throats come. If you're soft, I'm soft. If you're hard, I'm hard. And nobody in no fix ever seen me hisitate.

13. When there's danger, chrissake, my heart gets big and the whole world's a battlefield so don't wonder about that 'cause if you're a man you go where you want.

14. I'm a cowboy! So hear what I'm saying. To me, it's a small world, and could be bigger. Snakes don't bite me, the sun don't burn my head.

15. I was born like the little fishies at the bottom of the ocean. Nobody quits me what God give me. What I brung to this world, that's what I'm taking out.

16. My greatness is like the birds in the sky. I make no nest on this earth, 'cause there's too much sufferin' there and no body follows me when I take wing again.

17. Women? They come with too many arguments. Like those purty birds who jump from branch to branch, I make my bed in fields of clover, just the stars for my blanket.

18. So whoever's listenin', let me tell you of my woes. I don't fight, I don't kill . . . lest I have to. And with all that adversity, I only jump in what they treat me bad.

19. So listen to this story, the story of a persecuted cowboy. I was a good father, and a good husband, and yet now . . . they treat me like a thief.

Vicente Huidobro

CHILE, 1893–1948

Globe-Trotter

French

Your blue glance
  your blue glance
Many waves many rocks
  where do they all go?
In what port will I leave behind my song?
Wind makes the stars rotate
And the sailboat departs
In your trembling glance

My verses and years
Have wandered through here

In this sea sweet prairie
where all springs make peace
All my flowery boats
Have shipwrecked on this sea

Mariner of decline
  let us look at the sails
I shall never go to beaches without seagulls

Always standing
Mariner at the bottom of the sky
With open arms on the prow

The smoke of your pipe has inflated the clouds
And all the sky smells like your tobacco

  Look beyond
  Sad mariner
  From being a Christ
  On the masts

Let us raise our arms
Toward the sky born from water
Until that dawn forgotten by birds

The wind makes the stars rotate
And I follow her eyes newborn fish
Between the fingers a bit of azure
Sea foam in the shoes

The point in the horizon is my hat
And in all the beaches
My tie is a flag in the wind

Globe-trotter
I'm far from myself
Inside that fog I recall
(A memory that shines like a lamp
Orange in the hand)

I was at school, I was interned
And the summer went by
On the edge of your blue eyes.

Sor Juana Inés de La Cruz

MEXICO, 1648–1695

Misguided Men

Spanish

Stubborn men, who will chastise
a woman without cause,
oblivious that you're the source
of what you've criticized;

if your passion is so strong
that you elicit their disdain,
why do you wish they restrain
when you incite them to wrong?

You topple their defense,
and then, with gravity,
you credit sensuality
for what was won with diligence.

Your daring must be confronted,
for your sense is no less bogus
than the child who fears the ogre,
then weeps when is revolted.

Your presumptions are bound,
that for a wife you want Lucrece,
in lovers you prefer Thaïs,
thus seeking blessings be found.

What humor brings more fear,
which, without counsel to be found,
itself first the mirror ground
then lament it isn't clear?

With either favor or disdain
the selfsame purpose you achieve,
if they love, they are deceived,
if they don't, then you complain.

No woman will suit your taste
with circumspection as virtue:
ungrateful, she who loves you not,
yet she who does, is waste.

You men are such a stubborn breed,
appraised with ungodly rule,
the first you charge with being cruel,
the second, easy, you feed.

How might she bring you gains,
the one with love to extend?
If not willing, she'll offend,
and if willing, she inflames.

Amid anger and torment
your whimsy results in flair,
one is found who doesn't care:
then quickly your grievances vent.

So lovingly you bring her pain
that inhibitions run in fray;
why, after leading them astray,
should you wish without strain?

Who will greater guilt incur
when is passion that's misleading?
She who errs and heeds his pleading,
or he who pleads for her to err?

Who's is greater guilt therein
when all conduct will dismay:
she who sins and takes the pay,
or he who hires her to sin?

Why, for sins you're guilty of
do you still your blame debate?
Either love what you create
or create what you might love.

Were it not better to abstain,
and so, with finer stimulation,
obtain unforced admiration
of her you plotted to contain?

In such landscape to behold,
with your arms and arrogance,
in promise and deliverance
adjoin devil, flesh, and world.

Stay, Shadow

Spanish

Stay, shadow of my elusive prize
image of enchantment I most want,
fair illusion for whom I joyfully die,
sweet fiction for whom I painfully live.

If to the magnet of your charm's attraction
serves my breast of obedient steel,
why do you entice me with your flattery,
if you then will fool me with escape?

'Tis you can't boast in satisfaction
that I fell victim to your tyranny;
though while you fooled the straight bond

that your fantastic form constrained,
it matters little to fool arms and breast
if my fantasy holds you prisoner.

Darío Jamarillo Agudelo

COLOMBIA, 1947–

Love Poem 8

Spanish

Your tongue, your wise tongue that invents my skin,
your fire tongue that burns me,
your tongue that creates the instant of insanity, delirium
of the body in love
your tongue, sacred whip, sweet ember,
invocation of fire that takes me out of myself,
that transforms me,
your tongue of unmodest flesh,
your tongue of surrender that demands everything from me,
your tongue very mine,
your beautiful tongue electrifying my lips, making yours the body you have purified,
your tongue exploring and discovering me,
your gorgeous tongue also knowing how to say it loves me.

Vengeance

Spanish

Now you, turned into a poem,
imprisoned in verses naming you,
beautiful, unnamable, luminous,
now you, turned into a poem,
your body, brightness,
frost, word waste,
the poem almost your body
imprisoned in the poem,
turned into verses read in the living room,
your body that is past tense
and is this poem
poor vengeance.

Besik Kharanauli

GEORGIA, 1939–

We Should Dig Out Potatoes

Georgian

"We should dig out potatoes tomorrow!"
you told me,
pulling the chair close to the bed
where you were planning to place your clothes
after switching off the light. Acknowledging your words,
I turned my face
toward the wall;
I made it clear
I had other plans,
things to do next day.
I was fifteen.
The next day was Sunday
and I had my own projects.
Still, you made it clear:
we had to dig out potatoes.
Ready to sleep,
you turned your face
toward the wall,
and you went on,
attempting to convince me:
"A lot of work still needs to be done.
The weather is ripening.
Should the rain come fast enough, the potatoes will rot."
Like a bedtime kiss
and pat on the head,
you murmured:
"Aren't they good in winter,
toasted in ashes?"
Perhaps you meant to add a thought
or even offer a caress,
and not like the way
you joked with me—as if I were a kid—
while I was facing the wall.
Still, we silently agreed
on everything.

This happened long ago,
in Tianeti,
at this exact time of year,
mid-October.
The scene
returns to me just now,
in Tbilisi,
at midnight, while lying in bed
as I switch the light off,
and turn my face to the wall.
That evening, I was in desperate need
of a good night's sleep.
Yet as soon as I remembered,
my wakefulness was set
and I was overwhelmed by insomnia,
as usually happens to me
whenever I travel early the next day
or some kind of job awaits me.
All these years
and I still can't learn
how to put myself to sleep.
So now, wide awake, I write
with a pen given to me as a gift
by my own fifteen-year-old son
at a birthday party that never happened.
He too should get up early tomorrow,
although it's wishful-thinking
since only a rough shake
can rescue him from his morning sleep—
only yoked oxen can drag him
out of his slumber,
and only a herder
as damned as I am.

Our yard is less than half a hectare.
At one point, we planted potatoes on half of it
and corn and green beans on the other.
Only a small meadow in front of the house
remained for cattle, with a path
to guide the herd from cowshed to barn.
Oh, I still remember
how the cattle would graze the corn
near the hay
while my mother and I, at that time
strict guards,
moved them around twice a day.
After the war, the potato area shrank,
and we went back to planting yeast.
Mother convinced me that potatoes were like figs.
Then and after,
we would barter for onions or peaches
for a long time
with people from Kakheti.
Now, especially in the last few years,
we plant such a small amount of potatoes
that a person could till the whole field
in exchange for a bottle of liquor.
Still, digging out potatoes grants me a unique feeling:
accomplishment, discovery, joy.
It's easy to harvest when two people work together—
a shared venture:
one uses the spade,
the other pulls them out.

As my mother digs out the potatoes,
dusting the mud from the surface,
finding them hidden under the sand with her magician's fingers,
I lean on the spade's handle
and tell her a story.

Later, it's my turn to dig a new hole,
and she is the one to tell a story.
Back and forth, we go for hours,
just the two of us,
alone under the sun.
To keep our spirits,
neither anything embarrassing,
we just enjoy each other,
basking in the light and sensing the wind.
We dig out our past,
finding pieces of gold,
and airing them under the sun,
admiring them and letting them soothe us for four or five hours,
before burying them back until next year.

Yet sometimes we face moments of crisis
for example,
when I receive a letter from mother,
in which,
with a teacher's stern tone,
she asks me to visit her.
I am busy with other tasks,
or simply prefer to go elsewhere—
to a parallel Georgia
with vineyards,
figs and chestnut trees.
But no, I have to dig out potatoes.
I react angrily,
protesting and dispensing blame.
Is all this really important?
Is it not enough what we have already?
Two sacks for the whole year.
Is it worth the suffering?
In spring, you write to me

that we must seed the soil;
in autumn—we need to dig them out.
In spite of my rebellion,
I finally give up,
grab my possessions
and leave for Tianeti.

Last fall,
my son and I visited her.
It was my son's first business-like trip.
Mother was overjoyed:
the descendants were back.
She was so feeble in her joy,
more than she had ever been in her difficult life.
She ran aimlessly, up and down the stairs.
She rambled,
looking like a mischievous girl.
She had almost forgotten
we needed to dig out potatoes again.
Only a hundred seeds remained
but it didn't matter.

Half an hour later,
my son was lured away by friends.
Before leaving our yard, he glanced at us
and asked to go.
We told him it was fine. He is only fifteen.
Alert, his conscience
almost made him hesitate.

As soon as we finish storing the potatoes,
my mother and I
wash our hands
and shake off the dirt from our clothes.

As soon as she hurries into the kitchen,
evening arrives. It is cold.
I will huddle in something warm
and sit down on the front yard,
under the big apple tree.
The best view of our pasture is from there.
It reminds me of the land
that used to lavishly feed us
—I remember it all!—,
sacrificing, as if being our parents.
But at present, the yard has only one role left:
to entertain us
during those incomplete few months
when we travel from Tbilisi to Tianeti.
I begin thinking of our apple trees,
their past
their lives there . . .
The leaves are still hanging on the stems.
But the wind is on its way already.
I was thinking of the wind,
which has blown me away like a leaf.
At this very moment,
the entire universe entered the gate of the yard,
locking itself between fences,
and dressing itself in local clothes.
For a long time,
I played with the universe,
discussing, arguing,
until my son's cheerful, vigorous
calls ceased to be heard
from beyond the gates.

They scared the ghosts.

Our supper was once again sentimental.
"It's good to have dug them out,"
mother said.
"We didn't put off doing it.
If the rainy season begins soon, the soil will be drenched,
which would have rotten the potatoes."
I drank a couple of glasses of homemade liquor
and started convincing mother
that all was well in my personal life,
that I would come back next spring
so that we, you and I, could sow potatoes again.
Small beyond her age,
she listened to me
—to my nonsense—
and was about to respond, saying something vital,
when she changed her mind.
She had swallowed that thought with saliva.
She knows she can't talk lightly
about the earth,
life,
winter,
spring,
bread,
or potatoes.
Everything feels difficult:
arduous and muddled.

COTRANSLATED WITH GVANTSA JOBAVA

Juan Liscano

VENEZUELA, 1915–2001

Body of Love

Spanish

If appearance, mirage, if illusion of nothingness,
if deceit were the present triumph of your body,
my love would be deceit too, and its own deceit,
the soul, ay!, deceived with what I'm loving.
If ornament of Death, if mask of Her,
such arduous fire, such fair beauty;
I thus would love the truth of Death
in that vain ornament and that pure mask.
I want to lie to Time and I even want to fool myself
so as to save your form and immortalize your grace;
to loose myself, once found; already done, undo myself
along your certain confines and through your winged blood.
You are the flower that once again, my branches, betrays
with the soft prestige of your invisible aroma
and the ancient dawn returning to return me
the brief day flower that night strips off.
Because I'm the defeated winner of your body
and I surrender to the empire affirmed by its defeat,
since your body takes from me the victory I earned
and chains the fury of my blood to its wound.
Yes!; your precise body, arriving in morning, turbulent,
from a distant silence, perhaps sonorous echo,
of an empty universe, perhaps clear darkness:
voice found in my voices, form found in my eyes.
And its lively life surrounding my life
of murmuring shadows, of docile clarities
and green quiets and secret music,
in me, it defeats its death; my death doesn't reach it.
And while I know, surely—earth tells me—
that I'm made of death, and to Death I go,
with the flower of your body, liveliest flower, I deceive it
and deceive deceit, perhaps disillusioned.

Dulce María Loynáz

CUBA, 1902–1997

The Mirror

Spanish

The mirror hanging on the wall,
where I sometimes see myself in passing . . .
is a dead pond brought
into the house.
Corpse of a pond is the mirror:
still, rigid water containing
in itself remnants of color,
remembrances
of the sun, of shadow . . . —movable
edges of the horizon burning, passing by
in circles, returning, never
burning up . . . —vague
reminiscence that coalesced in the glass
and cannot return to the distant
land from where the pond was torn up,
still white
of moon and jasmine, still trembling
of rain and birds, its waters . . .
This is water tamed by death:
it's a ghost
of a living water that shined one day,
free in the world, lukewarm, suntanned . . .
Open to the happy wind that
made her dance . . . ! The water doesn't dance
anymore; it will not reflect
the suns of each day. It is barely reached
by the withered ray filtered through
the window.
In what cold did they freeze you for so long,
vertical pond, no longer spilling
your stream over the carpet, no longer
emptying your remote landscapes
in the living room and your spectral
light? Gray, crystallized water,

my mirror, where I saw myself
so distant
sometimes, where I feared being kept
inside forever . . . Detached
from myself, lost in the mud
of ash made of limbering starts . . .

Love Is . . . Spanish

To love the delicate grace
of the blue swan and the rose rose;
to love the light of dawn
and the stars opening
and the smiles prolonging themselves . . .
To love the tree's plenitude,
to love the music of water
and the sweetness of fruit
and the sweetness of sweet
souls . . . , to love what's lovable isn't love:
love is to turn oneself into a pillow
for the tiredness of every day;
to put the living sun in the anxious,
blind seed that lost its path
searching for light, imprisoned
in its soil, defeated
by its own soil.. Love is to untangle spider-webs
of roads in darkness:
Love is to be a road and a stop!
Love is this loving of what pains us,
what makes us bleed
inside . . .
It is to enter the heart
of night and guess
which is the star in gestation . . . The star's
hope! . . . To love is loving from the black root.
Love is to forgive, and more than
forgive, to understand . . .
Love is holding tight to the cross tight, and nailing
oneself to the cross,
and dying and resurrecting . . .

Love is to resurrect!

I Dream of Classifying . . .

Spanish

I dreamed of classifying
Good and Evil, like the wise men
classify butterflies:
I dreamed of pinning down Good and Evil
in the dark velvet
of a glass box . . .
Under the white
butterfly, a sign that read: "GOOD."
Under the black
butterfly, a sign that read: "EVIL."
But the white butterfly
wasn't Good, nor was the black butterfly
Evil . . . And between my two butterflies,
flying fresh, golden, infinite,
all the butterflies on earth! . . .

Leopoldo Lugones

ARGENTINA, 1874–1938

History of My Death

Spanish

I dreamed of death and it was quite simple:
a silk thread enwrapped me,
and each kiss of yours
tightened me less with every twist.
And each of your kisses
was a day;
and the time between two kisses
a night. Death is quite simple.
And little by little the fatal thread
unwrapped itself. I no longer controlled it
but for a single bit in between my fingers . . .
Then, suddenly, you became cold,
and no longer kissed me . . .
I let the thread go, and my life vanished.

Juan Carlos Marset

SPAIN, 1963–

Embraceable

Spanish

To Piedad Bonnett

Irreplaceable you,
voice, your empty
of my inconsolable
emptiness in you.
My irremediable you,
you, my mirror
of your reflection

in me. Unforced
into your silence,
silent voice of heartless
dream
between my body
and yours, undoing
this memory

of my embraceable you,
you, voice that strengthens
while banishing the angel
we gave ourselves
when we said
what might never have
happened to us.

José Martí

CUBA, 1853–1895

Two Homelands

Spanish

I have two homelands: Cuba and the Night.
Or are they one and the same? No sooner
does it's majesty, the sun, retire, that Cuba, with long veils,
and a carnation in hand, silently,
like a sad widow, appears before me.
I know that bleeding carnation
trembling in her hand! It's empty,
my chest is destroyed and empty,
where the heart once was. It's time
to begin dying. The night is
the right time to say goodbye. The light is bothersome
and so are human words. The universe
speaks better than man.
Like a flag
inviting us to battle, the candle's
red flame flickers. Too full of myself,
I open the windows. Silent,
plucking the carnation's leaves,
like a cloud darkening the sky,
Cuba, like a widow, passes by.

Kadya Molodowsky

BELARUS, 1894–1975

God of Mercy

Yiddish

1945

God of Mercy,
choose another people,
for a while.
We are exhausted of death and corpses,
we have run out of prayers,
for a while,
We have no more blood
to be sacrificed.
A desert is what our houses have become.
The earth is full of our tombstones,
there are no more lamentations,
no more songs of woe
in the old books.

God of Mercy,
make another land holy,
another Sinai.
We have filled every field and stone
with ashes, with holiness.
With our old,
and our young,
and our newborns
we have paid for each
letter of the Ten Commandments.

God of Mercy,
elevate your burning brow,
and look at the people of the world—
give them the prophecies and Days of Awe
who utter your words in every language—
teach them the deed,
the ways of perdition.

God of Mercy,
give us rags
of shepherds who tend sheep,
of blacksmiths with their hammer,
of washerwomen, cattle slaughters,
and even lower gifts.
And grant us one more gift,
God of Mercy,
take away the *Shekhinah* from our condition.

Eugenio Montejo

VENEZUELA, 1938–2008

Earthliness

Spanish

To be here on earth for years on end,
among the arriving clouds, with birds,
suspended from fragile hours.
On board, almost adrift,
closer to Saturn, much further,
while the sun turns around carrying us
and the blood traverses its deep universe
more sacred than all the planets.

To be here on earth: not further
than a tree, nor more inexplicable;
light in autumn, swollen in summer,
with what we are and are not, with shadow,
memory, desire till the end
(if there is an end) voice with voice,
one house after another,
no matter who is leading on earth, if someone might,
no matter who is waiting for it, if someone might,
breaking bread together
in two, three, four,
without forgetting the ant's leftovers
always traveling from remote stars
to arrive on time for our dinner
although the crumbs are meager.

Ithaca

Spanish

for an homage to C. Cavafis

Through this road one gets to Ithaca
and in its rumor of voices, steps, shadows,
any man is Ulysses.

Recorded among its stones is the map
of the land yearned for. Follow it.

The bird you are listening to sings in Greek;
don't translate it, it won't save you from the road.

Those clouds come from its sea, contemplate them;
the island's skies are purer.

Through this street, in any car,
one travels to Ithaca toward the north or south.
Fire is burning in the passer-bys' eyes,
their fast steps acknowledge exile.

Even if you don't move, like these trees
you shall reach Ithaca today or tomorrow.

It is written in the palm of your hand
like a deepening line,
day after day.

Even if you fall asleep, you shall wake up in Ithaca;
this valley's rain, it carries along everything
slowly, onto its doors.

It descends no more.
You can already announce your arrival to us, look for a hotel,
let your exile be swept by oblivion.

No man has crossed this street
who, in the end, doesn't reach his landscape.

Get your heart ready for arrival.

Once in its kingdom, show your magic.
It shall be the supreme challenge of exile.

No one lies to that ocean. The fury of its waves
turns everything into shipwreck. But don't let yourself be defeated.

Show us you were always Ulysses.

Álvaro Mutis

COLOMBIA, 1923–2013

Lament for the Death of Marcel Proust

Spanish

In what corner of your alcove, before which mirror,
behind what forgotten bottled of coughing,
did you make a pact?
With a truce fulfilled that took years, months,
weeks of asphyxia,
of interminable days of summer
lived through thick duvet covers,
searching, calling, rescuing
the intact seed of time,
building a durable labyrinth
where the habit loses its special energy,
its voracious extermination;
death lies in wait at the bottom of your bed,
sculpting in your millenarian face
your agony's lethal mask.
It sticks to your dark rabbi's hair,
digging the feverish well of your eye bags
and something of a dry flower, of light volcanic ash,
of a popper's washed-out bandage,
extends through your body
like a light, out-of-this world shroud
and an enduring foggy seal.
Now you see it standing, coming to you,
injuring you malignantly in the chest
and you ask Celeste to open the windows
where autumn beats like an injured beast.
But it no longer hears you, it doesn't understand you,
and, needlessly, it comes with its spinner's hurried fingers
to open even more the oxygen valves
and bring to you a bit of the air that evades you
and alleviate your supplicant's death.
Monsieur Marcel ne se rend comptre de rien,
she explains to your friends
who ask skeptically about your ailment

and you call her with the hoarse breathlessness of he who breathes
the last sight of life.
You extend your hands to the dry emptiness of the world,
you rip the skin of your throat,
your sweet eyes of yesteryears jump up
and for the last time your chest emerges
in a violent effort seeking to liberate
itself of the weight of the loss that awaits you.
Silence takes over your dominion,
While your precipitate yourself dizzily
toward the nostalgic limbo habituated,
in the edge of time, by your creatures.
Vague shadows cross your face
while you reclaim from death
a new portion of your affairs
and, erasing the disdain of a long agony,
your facial gestures of astute Babylonian hunters come up,
emerging from the bottom of the funeral waters
to show the world
the fertile endurance of your dream,
the ruin of time and the routine
of the fragile matter that makes time.

Pablo Neruda

CHILE, 1904–1973

Your Laughter

Spanish

Take bread away from me, if you wish,
take air away, but
do not take from me your laughter.

Do not take away the rose,
the lance flower that you pluck,
the water that suddenly
bursts forth in joy,
the sudden wave
of silver born in you.

My struggle is harsh and I come back
with eyes tired
at times from having seen
the unchanging earth,
but when your laughter enters
it rises to the sky seeking me
and it opens for me all
the doors of life.

My love, in the darkest
hour your laughter
opens, and if suddenly
you see my blood staining
the stones of the street,
laugh, because your laughter
will be for my hands
like a fresh sword.

Next to the sea in the autumn,
your laughter must raise
its foamy cascade,
and in the spring, love,

I want your laughter like
the flower I was waiting for,
the blue flower, the rose
of my echoing country.

Laugh at the night,
at the day, at the moon,
laugh at the twisted
streets of the island,
laugh at this clumsy
boy who loves you,
but when I open
my eyes and close them,
when my steps go,
when my steps return,
deny me bread, air,
light, spring,
but never your laughter
for I would die.

The Son

Spanish

Ah son, do you know, do you know
where you come from?

From a lake with white
and hungry gulls.

Next to the water of winter
she and I raised
a red bonfire
wearing out our lips
from kissing each other's souls,
casting all into the fire,
burning our lives.

That's how you came into the world.

But she, to see me
and to see you, one day
crossed the seas
and I, to clasp, her tiny waist,
walked all the earth,
with wars and mountains,
with sands and thorns.

That's how you came into the world.

You come from so many places,
from the water and the earth,
from the fire and the snow,
from so far away you journey
toward the two of us,
from the terrible love
that has enchained us,
that we want to know

what you're like what you say to us
because you know more
about the world we have you.

Like a great storm
we shook
the tree of life
down to the hiddenmost
fibers of the roots
and you appear now
singing in the foliage,
in the highest branch
that with you we reach.

Ode to Age

Spanish

I don't believe in age.
All old people
have in
their eyes
a child,
and children
sometimes
look at us with
the eyes of wise old people.
Shall we measure
life
in meters or kilometers
or months?
In length since birth?
How much
do you need to walk
until,
like everyone,
instead of walking on the surface,
we rest under the earth?
To the man, the woman
who performed
acts, goodness, strength,
love, tenderness,
to those who truly
flourished
alive
and matured in their nature,
let us not apply to them
the measure
of time
that perhaps is
something else, a mineral
mantle, a planetary

bird, a flower,
something else perhaps,
but not a measure.
Time, metal
or bird, large-stalk
flower,
stretch
widely
through men's lives,
flower them
and wash them
with
bright
water
or with hidden sun.
I proclaim you
path
and not shroud,
pristine
staircase
with steps
of air,
suit humbly
renewed
with longitudinal
springs.
Now,
time, I roll you up,
I deposit you in my
rustic box
and I leave off to fish
with your long thread
the fish of dawn!

Ode to the Andean Cordillera

Spanish

Once again, from up high,
flying over
the sky,
you appeared, white and obscure
cordillera of my homeland.
Before then, the great airplane
crossed great seas,
jungles, deserts.
Everything was symmetry,
everything was ready
on the earth's surface,
everything from above
was path,
until, in the middle
of heaven and earth,
your planetary snow
lodged itself,
freezing the towers of earth.
Volcanoes, scars,
caves,
ferruginous snows,
skinned
titanic heights,
heads of mountains,
feet of sky,
abyss of the abyss,
stabs
cutting
the terrestrial shell,
and the sun,
at seven thousand
meters above land,
hard like a diamond
on

the veins, the branches
of shadow and the snow
on the enraged
storm of the worlds,
stopping while boiling,
and the colossal
silence
imposed
its granite seas.

Homeland, the earth placed
on your slim hands
its toughest banner,
the Andean cordillera,
snowed blade, pristine solitudes,
stone and shiver,
and on your side
like an infinite flower the sea offers you
its spilt foam.
Oh sea, oh snow,
oh sky
of my small country,
to man, to the compatriot,
to the comrade
behind,
you shall give,
you shall give one day
the bread of your grandeur,
you shall unite it to the fate
of snow,
to the sacred splendor
of the sea and its energy.
Tough dwelling,
one day

you shall open up
delivering
the secret
fecundity,
the ray of your qualities,
and then
my small
compatriot,
injured severely in your kingdom,
wretched
in its own fortitude,
ragged in its confines of gold,
it shall receive
the treasure
while conquering it,
defending the snow of its star,
multiplying the sea and its bunches,
extending the silence of fruit.
Cordillera, school
of stone,
I celebrate
your magnitude
in this hour,
your toughness,
the cold candelabra
of your elevated
solitudes of snow,
the night,
motionless estuary,
navigating
on
the stones of your sleep,
the translucent
day

on your head
and on it, on the snowed
hair
of the world,
the condor
raising
his powerful
wings,
his dignified
flight
over vigorous heights.

Ode to Ángel Cruchaga

Spanish

Ángel, I remember
in my childhood,
southern and shaken
by rain and wind,
suddenly
your wings,
the flight
of your sparkling poetry,
the starry
tunic
filling the night, the roads,
with phosphoric resplendence,
you were
a pulsating river
full of fish,
you were
the silvery tail
of a green mermaid
crossing the sky
from west
to east,
the shape of light
gathered
in your wings, and the wind
allowing rain and black leaves to fall
on your clothes.
So it was
far away,
in my childhood,
but your poetry
not only
a step made of many wings,
not only
wandering stone,

meteor
dressed in colors of amaranth and white lily,
was and still is,
but a flowering plant,
monument
to human tenderness,
orange blossom
with roots
in man.
That's why,
Ángel,
I sing to you,
I've sung to you
the way I've sung to all pure things,
metals,
waters,
wind!
Everything becomes a lesson to live,
growth
through hardship and sweetness,
as in your poetry, the infinite
bread pregnant with the tears
of your passion, the noble
fragrant woods
your divine hands shape.
Ángel,
you, owner
of the widest jasmine trees,
allow your younger
brother to leave on your chest
these branches with rain
and roots.
I leave them in your book
so it becomes pregnant

with peace, transparency, and beauty,
living in the corolla
of your adamantine nature.

Ode to the Apple

Spanish

You, apple,
I want
to celebrate you
by filling
my mouth
with your name,
by eating you.
You're always
new like nothing else,
or no one,
always
as if just fallen
from Paradise:
plentiful
and pristine,
reddened cheek
of aurora!
How unappealing
are
the fruits of earth
compared
to you,
the grainy grapes,
the gloomy
mangos,
the seedy
plums, the submarine
figs:
you are pure ointment,
fragrant bread,
cheese
of vegetation.
When we bite
into your rounded innocence,

for an instant
we return
to being
newly created creatures again:
somehow we remain apple.
I want
a total
abundance, the multiplication
of your family,
I want
a city,
a republic,
a Mississippi River
of apples,
and on its shores
I want to see
the entire
population
of the world
united, reunited,
in the simplest act on earth:
biting an apple.

Ode to the Dictionary

Spanish

Back like an ox, beast
of burden, systematic
dense book:
young
I ignored you, I was visited
by smugness
and I thought myself complete,
and plump like a
melancholy toad
I proclaimed: "I receive
words
directly
from the roaring Mount Sinai.
I shall reduce
forms into alchemy.
I am a magus."
The great magus said nothing.
The Dictionary,
old and heavy, with its scruffy
leather jacket,
was silent,
its test tubes undisplayed.
But one day,
after having used it
and perused it,
after
declaring it
a useless and anachronistic camel,
when for long months, without protest,
it served as an armchair
and a pillow,
it rebelled, and planted itself
in my doorstep,
it expanded, shook its leaves

and nests,
it moved the elevation of its foliage:
it was
tree,
neutral,
generous,
apple tree, *apple orchard*, or *apple blossom*,
and the words
shining in their inexhaustible cup,
opaque or sonorous,
fertile in the lodging of language,
charged with truth and sound.
I turn
to a single one
of its
pages:
Cape
Cartridge
how wonderful
to pronounce these syllables
with air,
and further on,
Capsule
hollow, awaiting oil or ambrosia,
and near them
Captivate Capture Capuchin
Carousel Carpathian
words
slippery as smooth grapes
or exploding in the light
like blind seeds awaiting
in the storehouse of vocabulary
alive again and given life:
once again the heart is burning them.

Dictionary, you are not
tomb, sepulcher, coffin,
tumulus, mausoleum,
but preservation,
hidden fire,
plantation of rubies,
living eternity
of essence,
granary of language.
And it is wonderful
to harvest in your fields
a lineage
of words,
the severe
and forgotten
sentence,
daughter of Spain,
hardened
like a plow blade,
fixed in its limit
of antiquated tool,
preserved
in its exact beauty
and the immutability of a medallion.
Or another
word
we find hiding
between lines
that suddenly seems
as delicious and smooth in our mouths
as an almond
or as tender as a fig.
Dictionary, let one
of your thousand hands, one

of your thousand emeralds,
a
single
drop
of your virginal springs,
one grain
of
your
magnanimous granaries
fall
at the right moment
on my lips,
the thread of my pen,
into my inkwell.
From the dense and sonorous
depths of your jungle,
give me,
when I need it,
a single birdsong, the luxury
of a bee,
the fallen fragment
of your ancient wood perfumed
by an eternity of jasmine,
one
syllable,
one tremor, one sound,
one seed:
I am made of earth and with words I sing.

Ode to the Flowers of Datitla

Spanish

Under the pines, the earth concocts
small unsullied things:
slim grasses
from whose threads
minuscule lanterns hang,
mysterious capsules
plump with lost air,
and shadows
are different there,
filtered
and flowery,
long green needles scattered
by the wind attacking and disheveling
the hair of pine trees.
On the sand
stand
fragmentary petals,
calcified bark,
blue pieces
of dead wood,
leaves the patience
of beetle-like woodcutters
moves around, thousands
of minimal cups
left behind by the eucalyptus
over
your
cold and fragrant
silhouette
and herbs
are
like flannels
planted
with the softness

of gloves,
sticks
of proud spines,
wiry pavilions
of dark acacia
and flowers the color of wine,
bulrush, heads of corn,
thickets,
harsh stems united like
locks on the sand,
round
stems
of somber green
cut with scissors,
and amidst the tall yellowness
suddenly
while shooting skyward
a rustic circumference of gold,
the tiger-flower flourishes
with three tongues
of ultraviolet love.

Datitla sand
united to the open statuary
of La Paz, in the first
waves of the gray Atlantic,
deliver beloved solitude,
you not only return me
to the penetrating
smell and movement
of sea pine,
not only
to the honey of love and its deliciousness,
but to the purest circumstances

on earth:
to the dray and wild
Flora of the Sea, Air,
and Silence.

Ode to Gratitude

Spanish

Gracias to the word
that is thankful.
Thanks to *gracias*
for the extent
to which this word
melts snow or iron.

The world appeared threatening
until soft
goes *gracias*
from lip to lip
as a clear-headed pen,
or sweet like a sugar petal,
or whispering,
barley being voiced,
and a being became man again
and not a window,
some clarity
entered the forest,
able to sing amidst the leaves.
Gracias, you're a pill
against
scorn's biting oxides,
light against the altar of harshness.

Perhaps
you were also carpet
against the most distant men.
Passengers
were disseminated
in nature
and then
in the jungle
of unknown men,

merci,
while the frantic train
switches countries,
erases borders,
spasivo,
near the sharp-cusped
volcanoes, cold and fire,
thanks, yes, *gracias*, and then
the earth becomes a table,
a word swept it clean,
plates and cups shine,
forks jingle
and plains resemble tablecloths.

Thanks, *gracias*,
may you travel and return,
rise up
and come down.
It's understood that you,
gracias word,
don't permeate all things,
but where
your small petal
appears,
proud daggers hide away
and a penny's worth of smiles emerges.

Ode to Guatemala

Spanish

Guatemala,
today
I sing
to you.

Without reason,
without purpose,
this morning
your name
appeared
entangled
in my mouth,
green dew,
morning freshness,
I remembered
the lianas
tying
with their
rustic cord
the sacred treasure
of your jungle.

I remembered in your heights
the invisible river-beds
of your waters,
sonorous
secret turbulence,
corollas fastened
to the foliage,
a bird
like a sudden sapphire,
the overflowing sky,
full like a cup
of peace and transparency.

Above
a lake
with a name of stone.
Amatitlán it is called.
Waters, waters from heaven
filled it,
waters, waters of starts
gathered together
in the frightening depth
of a dark emerald.
In its margins
the tribes
of Mayab
survive.

Tender, tender
idolaters
of honey, secretaries
of heavenly bodies,
beaten
winners
of the most archaic enigma.

It is lovely to see
the dressed-up splendor
of its small villages,
they dared
to continue carrying
resplendent tunics,
yellow embroideries,
scarlet panties,
the colors
of the aurora.
In days gone by

the soldiers
of a mourning Castile
buried America,
and to this day
the American
man
wears the frock-coat
of a notary from Extremadura,
Loyola's
cassock
Inquisitive
Spain,
a purgatory,
sheathed the sounds
and colors,
the lineage of America,
the pollen, the happiness,
and left us behind
its suit of Salamancan sorrow,
its suit of armor
of inexorable rag.

Only in you does
the submerged color survive,
the plumage, radiant,
survive,
your large-mouthed pitcher
survives in torrents,
profound
Guatemala,
you were not buried
by the successive wave
of death,
the invading foreign

wings,
funeral cloths
did not succeed
in drown your corolla
of glittering flower.

I saw in Quetzaltenango
the fertile
crowd
in the market,
the baskets
of plaited love,
the ancient
sorrows,
the fabrics
of turbulent color,
red race,
vessel heads,
profiles of
metallic white lily,
grave glances, white
smiles like a heron's
flight on the river,
feet the color of copper,
people
of the earth,
dignified
Indians like
a pack of monarchs.

So much
smoke fell
on their countenance, so much
silence

they did not speak
but with corn, with tobacco,
with water,
they were
threatened by tyranny
even in their enrooted territories,
or in the coast
by invading North Americans
who devastated the land,
taking the fruit with them.

And now
Arévalo elevated
a handful of soil
for them,
just a handful
of germinating dust, that's all,
that's all, Guatemala,
a minuscule
and fragrant
fragment of land,
a few seeds
for the poor people,
a plough
for the peasants.
And that's why
when Arbenz
brought in justice,
and with the land gave out rifles,
when the
feudal
coffee growers
and the adventurers of Chicago
found

in the house of government
not a despotic puppet,
but a man,
then
fury settled in,
they filled
newspapers
with communiqués:
Guatemala was burning.

Guatemala wasn't burning.
On top was Lake
Amatitlán, quiet with a centuries-old
sight,
looking toward the sun and the moon shined,
Dulce River
carried
primordial waters,
fish and birds,
its jungle,
its beat
from the primordial aroma of America,
the pines in their heights
murmured,
and the simple people
like sand and flour
succeeded, for the first time,
to see hope
face to face.

Guatemala,
I sing to you today,
I sing your past misfortunes
and your hope.

I sing your beauty.
But I want my love
to defend you.
I know
those who prepare a tomb for you
like the one they dug for Sandino.
I know them. Don't expect
piety from your executioners.
Today they get ready
By killing fishermen,
assassinating fish in the island.
They are implacable. But
you, Guatemala, are
a fist and a handful
of American dust with seeds,
a small handful
of hope.
Defend them, defend us,
we
today only with my song,
tomorrow with my people and my song
we shall arrive
to tell you "Here we are,"
small sister,
warm heart,
we are ready now
to bleed to
defend you,
because in the dark hour
you were
the honor, the pride,
the dignity of America.

Ode to the Inconsequential Day

Spanish

Silver fish
with orange
tail,
day of the sea,
on each hour
you changed
your clothes,
the sand
was blue,
azure
was your tie,
on a cloud
your fee
were foam
and then
the green flight
of the rain
over the pine trees
was total:
an iron spell
swept
the western
hopes,
the last or first
swallow
shined white and blue
like a revolver,
like a nocturnal watch
the sky only
preserved a platinum
minute hand,
well-rounded and black the sea
covered its heart
with velvet

suddenly showing
the snowy ring
or the curled
rose in its radiant delirium.

Restlessly fixated
I saw
all this
from my window
changing my shoes
to go through the sand
full of gold
or sink in the humidity, amidst the leaves
of red eucalyptus,
curbed like Corinthian daggers,
and I could not
know
if the Rainbow
like a Mexican flag
grew toward Cartagena
was an announcement
of sweet light
or a tower of darkness.
A fragment
of cloud
like the remnant
of a flying shirt
rotated
in the last threshold
of celestial panic.

The day
trembled from side to side,
a lightning

ran like an alligator
amidst the clothing
of the jungle
and in one shot the entire dew fell down
disappearing in the dust
of the savage hair-band.
Between the clouds and the earth,
white, flat, stubborn,
and a green and tall
rooster
like a pine
sang, sang
as if he was threshing
all the corn in the world:
a river,
a blond river
entered through the darkest
windows
and not the night, not the tempestuous
indecisive clarity
established over the earth,
but simply
another day,
a day.

Ode to Jean Arthur Rimbaud

Spanish

Now,
this October
you will turn
a hundred,
harrowing friend.
May I speak
to you?
I'm alone,
through my window
the Pacific breaks
its eternal threatening thunder.

It is night.

The burning firewood throws
over the oval
of your old portrait
a fugitive ray.
You are a child
of twisted locks,
sour mouth.
I apologize
if I talk to you
the way I do, the way
I trust you would be,
if I talked of marine water
and burning firewood,
of simple things and simple beings.

They tortured you
and burnt your soul,
they imprisoned you
in the walls of Europe
and furiously
you would bang

the doors.
And when you were
finally
able to depart
you were injured,
injured and mute,
dead.

Quite soon, other poets
abandoned
a raven, a swan,
a willow,
a lyre's petal,
you left behind a ghost
ripped
who curses
and spits
and walks
still
without direction,
without fixed address,
without number,
through the streets of Europe,
returning to Marseille,
with African sand
in his shoes,
urgent
like a shiver,
thirsty,
bloody,
with his pockets broken,
defiant,
lost,
wretched.

It is not true
you stole the fire,
you ran
with celestial fury
and with an ultraviolet
chest of stones
from hell,
it is not so,
I don't believe it,
you we denied
simplicity, the house,
wood,
you were rejected,
doors were closed for you,
and therefore you flew,
irate archangel,
to remote
lodgings,
and coin by coin,
sweating and bleeding
your height
you wanted
to accumulate the necessary
gold
for simplicity, for the key,
for the virtuous wife,
for the son,
for your chair,
bread and beer.

In your time
over the spider webs
wide
as an umbrella

the twilight was shutting down
and oil blinkered
drowsily.
You passed by the Commune,
red child,
and your poetry gave
blazes of fire
still ascending while it punishes
the walls
used in executions.
With eyes
like a dagger
you drilled
the decayed
shadow,
war, the wandering
cross of Europe.
That is why today, with a distance
of one hundred years,
I invite you
to the simple
truth unattained
by your hurricane-shaped forehead,
I invite you to America,
to our rivers,
to the breath of the moon
over the cordillera,
to the emanation
of workers,
to the extended homeland
of the people,
to the electrified
Volga River
with grape bunches and wheat shoots,

to what man
conquered without mystery,
with force
and blood,
with one hand and with the other,
with millions
of hands.

You were driven crazy,
Rimbaud, you were condemned
and hastened
into hell.
You deserted the germ's
cause, you buried
the flame
and in desert-like solitude
you served
your sentence.
Today it is simpler, we are
countries, we are
peoples,
guaranteeing the growth of poetry,
the distribution of bread, the patrimony
of oblivion. Now
you would not be
solitary.

Ode to the Month of August

Spanish

I once again return
to the clear
amidst the land,
to look
and touch
wild stones,
sand, branches, moon.
Southern August,
August
clean and cold,
your column
raises
from the earth to the sky
and you are crowned
by the starry rocks,
the night of sapphire.

Oh
clear
winter,
I see
your rectangle flourish
in a
single
rose,
the snow,
and white, azure, your pure
geometry
teaches me
an open
lesson:
the world is without leaves,
without beat,
deprived of everything
that dies:

it is only
stone and cold,
book naked of crystal where
the long letters of light ascend.

August without
streets, without
numbers,
August without shoes
walking
toward pain,
I return
to your solitude
not
to
be drawn
in it,
but
to
wash myself in your waters,
so in me
the cold moon
might slide,
and step on stones
in the forests, fallen
leaves
of August, and everything has
a stainless extension,
sky flavor, height
of a youthful heart under the rain.

Oh
full potency,
clarity
striped

from the earth,
I
love
your
abstract
peace
on the roads.
I want
to be
alone
in the middle
of the August light
and hence
see,
without blood,
life
for once:
see it
like
an uninhabited
and beautiful
ship,
without more aroma and the marine air
or the invisible air of sour rosemary.
Step by step,
without a thing:
there is nothing but
moon and snow.
And I wander
even without myself,
finally,
in the clearest
clarity of the earth!

Ode to the Moon

Spanish

Clock of the sky,
you measure
the celestial eternity,
one white
hour,
one century
sliding
on your snow,
meanwhile
the earth,
entangled,
is humid,
warm:
the hammers
hit,
the tall ovens
burn,
the petroleum
shakes in its plate,
man searches, hungry,
for matter,
he corrects
his banner,
siblings gather,
walk,
hear,
cities
emerge,
bells
sing
in the heights,
cloths are woven,
transparency
jumps

onto the crystals.
Meanwhile,
jasmine
or snowy
light,
moon,
bright clear,
tall,
action made of platinum,
gentle
dead,
you slide
through the night
without us knowing
who
your men are,
if you have
butterflies,
if in the morning
you sell
sweet bread,
white-star milk,
if you are
made of glass,
of orange cork,
if you breathe,
if in your meadows
beveled, fragile
serpents flow.

We want
to bring you near,
we look
at your impeccable

whiteness
until we're blind,
we adjust
the telescope in the mountain
and set the eye
until we fall asleep:
you don't talk,
you don't undress,
you don't light
a single bonfire,
you look
to the other side,
you count,
you count
the time
of night,
gentle
tic
tac,
gentle
tac
tic tac
like a drop on the snow,
round,
clock of water,
corolla
of time,
submerged
in the sky.

It won't be that way,
it won't always be,
I promise,
in the name

of all
the poets
that loved you
uselessly:
we shall open
your peace of pallid stone,
we shall enter
in your subterranean light,
fire
will be lit up
in your dead eyes.
We will inseminate
your frozen statue,
we will harvest
wheat
and birds
in your forehead,
we will navigate
in your white ocean.
And then
you will mark
the hours
of men,
in the heights
of the sky:
you will be
ours,
petals
of women
will be found
in your snow,
discovery of men,
and you will not be a useless
nocturnal

watch,
magnolia
of the tree of night,
but only
legume,
only cheese,
celestial cow,
spilt
udder,
spring
of milk,
useful
like the head of corn,
boundless,
reigning
and necessary.

Ode to the Murmur

Spanish

Verses of love, of mourning,
of cholera or moon,
are attributed to me:
of the kind I go on making
with labor,
apples and happiness,
people say they aren't mine,
that the verses show the influence
of Pitiney, of Papo,
of Sodostes.
Ah, what are we to do!
Life
kept on placing a dove
in my hand,
and another.
I learned to fly
and taught
while flying.
From the celestial sky,
I understood the duties
of the earth.
I saw the happenings
of men
with more clarity than the bitter
flight
of birds.
I loved the soil, I placed
in my heart the transparency
of moving water,
I formed,
from mud and wind, the vessel
of my constant song.
And then
I began to conquer a human family

from the towns,
houses,
ports
and mines,
I resisted poverty
with the poor.
I lived with my brothers.

Then
each attack of black wave,
each
heavy
slap of life
against my poor bones
was the sonorous toll of the bell,
and I became a bell ringer,
the bell ringer
of earth
and men.
Now
I am a bell ringer.
I hold the rope
with my soul.
The earth
makes my heart
tremble
with sound.
I climb, I traverse mountains,
I descend,
I share
the alarm, the happiness,
the hope.
Because
when

I'm tired perhaps,
when I sleep,
when I go out to drink with friends
the wine
of the lands that I love, and I defend others,
why do you persecute me, unhinged,
with a stone,
with a donkey's jawbone.
Why do you want me frightened,
when no one
has been able
to silent me until now?
Do you believe
that by placing a slippery apple's peel
on the street,
or on your far-flung
production of saliva,
you might be able
to stop my bell song
and my bell-ringer's vocation?
It is time
for us to understand each other:
go to bed early,
making sure the tailor is paid
by his mother and brother-in-law.
Let me
climb the staircase toward the bell:
while the sun burns in the cold,
and the bread
is still warm
in the inns.
It is daybreak,
and I, with my bell,
with my song,

wake up and wake you up.
That's my task
—even if I don't want to—:
to wake
you up and those who are asleep;
to convince darkness
that light has arrived.
This
is easy
to do,
it is pleasant,
like dispensing bread on the street,
so easy even I can do it,
singing like I sing,
sonorous like moving water,
and, like a bell ringer,
inexorable.

Ode to the Names of Venezuela — Spanish

The plains, once again burned
in February.
Venezuela is in flames
its paths divide
the extensive blaze,
the fertilizing light
dismantles the wealth
of its shadow.
I walk across the road,
while the planet
grows on each of my sides,
from Barquisimento
to Acarigua.
Like a hammer,
the sun
touches
the branches,
nails
celestial nails
onto the earth,
studies the corners
and like a rooster curls up
its plumage
over the green tiles of Barinas,
over the eyelids of Suruguarpo.

Your names, Venezuela,
the buried
rivers,
water, battles,
the somber
link between the jaguar and the cordillera,
the plumage
of unknown birds
in concordance with the jungle,

words
barely
uttered
perhaps made of pen or pollen,
or the tough
names of lance or stone:
Aparurén, Guasipati, Canaima,
Casiquiare, Mavaca,
And, further away, Maroa,
where the rivers under the darkness
fight with spears,
drag your existence.
wood, space, blood,
toward the iron foam of the Atlantic.

The names of Venezuela:
fragrant and assured,
running like water
over dry land,
illuminating
the face
of the earth
like the Aranguaney when raising
its pavilion of yellow kisses.

Ocumare:
you are eye, foam and pearl.
Tocuyo: child of flour.
Siquisique, you slide
like wet and odorous soap.
And, if I needed to choose, the sun
would be born with the name of Carora;
water would be born in Cabudare;
the sleeping night in Sabaneta.

In Chiriguare, in Guay, in Urucure,
in Coro, in Bucarai, in Moroturo—
these are the regions
of an assorted Venezuela
I continue to traverse.
And this is her treasure:
the ardent seeds of her names,
which I have now planted in my own far-away land.

Ode to Night

Spanish

Behind
the day,
in each stone and tree,
behind each book,
night,
you gallop and labor,
or rest,
waiting until your withdrawn roots
develop your flower and foliage.
Like
a flag
you flutter in the sky
until you fill not only
the hills and seas,
but the smallest cavities,
the tired peasant's
iron eyes,
the black coral
of the human mouths
given to dreaming.
You run free
over the savage course
of rivers,
covering secret paths, night,
depths of loves star-stricken
by the naked bodies,
crimes splashing
with the scream of a shadow,
meanwhile trains
run, the stokers
throw nocturnal coal to the red fire,
the busy statistics employee
has immersed himself in a forest
of petrified pages,

the baker kneads
whiteness.
Night also sleeps
like a black horse.
It rains
from north to south,
over the grand
trees of my country,
over the roofs
of corrugated metal,
the night's song
is heard,
the metal of the singing spear
is made of rain and darkness,
and stars and jasmine
guard
from the darkness above,
signs
we will understand
little by little
at the speed of centuries.
Night,
night of mine,
night of the entire world,
you have something
inside you, round
like a child
about to be born, like
a bursting
seed,
it is the miracle,
it is the day.
You are more beautiful
because with your darker blood

you feed to the poppy being born,
because you labor with eyes closed
so eyes can open,
so water might sign,
so our lives might come back to life.

Ode to Simplicity

Spanish

Simplicity, I ask you:
were you always with me?
Or am I finding you again
on the chair, seated?
Now
they don't want to accept me
along with you,
they look at me with suspicion,
they ask me who
the red-head is.
The world,
while we were finding
and recognizing each other,
was filling up with gloomy
idiots,
with children of fruit as full
of words
as dictionaries,
so full of wind
like gut wanting to play
a trick on us
and, now that we're back
after so many trips,
our poetry
is out of tune.
Simplicity, how terrible what's
happening to us:
they don't want to greet us
in the classrooms,
the cafés are full
of the most exquisite
child molesters,
and you and I look at each other,
we aren't wanted.

Then
we leave
for the sand,
for the forests,
at night
darkness is new,
the new-washed stars
shine, the sky
is a field of tumid
clover, shaken
by its somber
blood.
In the morning
we go
to the bakery,
the bread is lukewarm, like a breast,
the world
smells of this freshness
of newly baked bread.
Romero, Ruíz, Nemesio,
Rojas, Manuel Antonio,
bakers.
How alike are
bread and baker,
how simple is the earth
in the morning,
later is even simpler,
and at night
it is transparent.
That's why
I look
for names
in the grass.
What is your name?

I ask
a corolla
that, suddenly
stuck to the soil amid poor stones,
burned like lightning.
And thus, simplicity, we start
becoming acquainted
with the hidden beings, the secret
valve of other metals,
looking at the beauty of the leaves,
conversing with men and women
who are remarkable only because
they are who they are.
And you enrapture me
with everything
and everyone, simplicity.
I go with you,
surrendering to the torrent
of clear water.
And, therefore, they protest:
Who is she
who is with the poet?
We certainly
don't want anything to do
with that country girl.
But if it's air, it's she
the air I breathe.
I didn't know or remember her.
If they saw me
before
walking with mysterious
odalisques,
they were but gloomy
slips.

Now,
my love,
water,
tenderness,
luminous light and translucent
shadow,
simplicity,
are at my side, helping me to be born,
teaching me
to sing again,
truth, virtue, waterfall,
crystalline victory.

Ode to Things

Spanish

I love crazy things,
crazily.
I enjoy tongs,
scissors.
I adore
cups,
rings,
soup spoons,
not to mention, of course,
the hat.

I love
all things,
not only
the grand ones
but
the
infinitely
small,
the thimble,
spurs,
plates,
flower vases.

Ay, soul of mine,
the planet
is gorgeous,
full
of pipes
taken
by hand
amid the smoke,
of key rings,
salt shakers,

in short,
everything
made
by the hand of man, all things:
the curves of a shoe,
fabric,
the new birth
of gold
without blood,
eyeglasses,
nails,
brooms,
clocks, compasses,
coins, the soft
softness of chairs.

Ay, how many
pristine
things
man
has built:
of wool,
wood,
glass,
ropes,
marvelous
tables,
ships, staircases.
I love
all
things,
not because they
blaze
or are fragrant,

but because
I don't know,
because
this ocean is yours,
is mine:
buttons,
wheels,
small
forgotten
treasures,
feathered fans
on whose feathers
love spread
its orange blossoms,
cups, knives,
scissors,
everything rests
on the handle, in the contour,
the trace
of fingers,
a remote hand
lost
in the most forgotten of oblivions.

I wander through
houses,
elevators,
touching things,
spotting objects
I secretly covet:
one because it chimes,
another because
it is as soft
as the softness of a hip,

another for its color of deep water,
another for the thickness of its velvet.

Oh irrevocable
river
of things,
it should not be said
that I loved
only
fish,
or the jungle plants and the prairie,
that I not only
loved
what jumps, ascends, survives, sighs.
It isn't true:
many things
told me everything.
They not only touched me
or were touched by my hand,
but they accompanied
my existence
to such an extent
that they lived with me
and were so full of life for me
that they lived with me half a life
and would live with me for half a death.

Ode to the Watermelon

Spanish

Tree of summer,
intense,
invulnerable,
is all blue sky,
yellow sun,
exhaustion dripping.
It's a sword above the roads,
a burnt shoe
in the cities:
clarity and the world
overwhelm us,
hit us
in the eye
with dust,
with sudden blows of gold;
they harass
our feet
with thorns,
with heated stones,
and the mouth
suffers
more than all the toes:
the throat
is thirsty,
the teeth,
the lips and tongue:
we want
to drink waterfalls,
the blue night,
the pole.
Just then
the coolest of all planets
crosses the sky,
the rounded, supreme
and celestial watermelon.

It's the fruit from the tree of thirst.
It's the green whale of summer.

The dry universe,
suddenly
marked
by this firmament
of coolness,
allows
the fruit
to drop:
its hemispheres open,
showing a flag
—green, white, scarlet—
dissolving itself
in cascades, sugar,
delight!

Water, coffer,
placid fruit
queen,
warehouse
of depth,
earthly moon!
Oh, purity
incarnate,
rubies fall apart
in your abundance.
We would like
to bite you,
sinking
the face,
the hair,
the soul

into you!
Thirsty,
we see you
like a mine or mountain
of splendid food,
but
you transform
between our teeth and desire
into
fresh light that unleashes us,
becoming
a spring
that touches us,
singing.
And then,
you're weightless
in the all-embracing
siesta,
only
passing by,
and your great heart of cold coal
is transformed into water
contained in a single drop.

Andrés Neuman

ARGENTINA / SPAIN, 1977–

Genesis, COVID-19

Spanish

And the Pope said amen in the empty square
and no one answered from the clouds
and no one answered from the mirror
because all voices were beneath the ground
sweetly cradled to cease existence.
And the Stock Exchange swelled its lung
and counted the oxygen in coins
and rerouted its wind toward some islands
sewn to the sea with sutured wounds
only for lizards and exceptions.
And all countries became one
but specially themselves
since many needed to choose
between virus and bread and a few saved
a piece of future in the freezer.
And supermarkets were crowded
with animals in search of animals
with families in white that grazed
in a field of alcohol paper and plastic
and gloves keying the fear code.
And each hospital became tempest
and roofs rained and doors flew
and the thread of life became clear-cut
and truth came and went in hallways
without being asked any questions.
And grandparents could see
with skin like fishing nets
and hands stained with memory
and eyes blinded by lucidity
their rights turn into numbers.
And technology was flesh
in those who already had it and ghost
in those with only body
and we sang rhyming songs

promising never to forget.
And very soon our voices went quiet
in the usual places in multiple corners
with a fly's buzz in that devil's limbo
which is the border between song and silence
between mourning and amnesia.

Antonia Palacios

VENEZUELA, 1904–2001

That Obscure Animal of Dream (fragment)

Spanish

Many are the doors, many the crevices, and I can't quite go through. I bend myself with my primordial childhood, I become flexible, slim, impalpable, and I can't go through. I submerge myself in space, and I can't quite go through. I retreat, I try another place, another hideout. I rescue the air that is no longer the same. I turn around not to see. I hold my breath, my tortured breath. While I look for another exit. There the place sinks, a place without borders, I can almost touch it, and I can't quite go through. A dense lethargy creeps over my body, I foresee at a distance the sheets of heaven. I evoke the other time, the one of deep sleeplessness and that obscure animal of dream.

Writings of Eviction (fragment)

Spanish

I am dying. I am dying a slow death, silent, without noise. I am dying without dying. I am full of deaths. Deaths that pass by like shadows in front of my face. Deaths that run away and I can't reach. How to reach my own unique death? How to select it among so many deaths pestering me? I am dying of death as an only companion and death enters my house, steps on my rugs, touches the windows, silences my bells. I am dying of a harsh death, implacable. A death that skins me, turning my living flesh into dead flesh. I am dying of a thick death, violent, a death playing with my breath the game of death, and takes it and abandons it, it unties it and ties it, it takes it to its limits, it returns it to its beginning. A death that injures me without bloodshed and slowly empties my guts. I'm dying . . . And suddenly it seems as if death enlightens. That the dream of life is only a shadow, that the breath of life is a dead blow, empty racket of the shriek of love. That this vestments palpitating is only trembles and becomes still while embraced by death. And suddenly it seems as if I am no longer dying. As if I've reached death without dying.

João Pinto Delgado

PORTUGAL, 1580–1653

Leaving Egypt

Portuguese

In this fierce Egypt
of my sin, where my soul
suffers the tyrannical servitude
of your divine flame,
Master, send me a ray
of holy inspiration to be my guide
and let the light of your burning love
call upon me in the desert, never coursing
the mundane memory:
naked, in the blind veil of error,
all past habits left behind,
I joyfully ascend to contemplate your glory—
my being, by miraculous effect,
becoming a sovereign object.

Gonzalo Rojas

CHILE, 1916–2011

André Breton Turns a Hundred and Is Fine

Spanish

The time Breton died we all got together
to dance. For Nadja!, we said,
throwing the cups into the air
against the stars, and he looked
at the farce and wound his watch
made of dust: "It's because there's no Eternity,
dear friends, it's because there's no Eternity."

Elizabeth Schön

VENEZUELA, 1921–2007

From the Ancient Laborer I (fragment)

Spanish

The man dresses up
with the untouchable suit
of the ancient laborer . . .
that's where his clothes fit him better
because it is there where his saddlebags were born
and that fluorescent color of the clothing
extended over the round space
of centuries and seconds.
He contemplates the extremes edges
of sierras and clouds.
He fixes his sight in each bunch
in each closeness and distance
and neither on the plateaus nor in the tablelands
nor further away in the crest
in the openings in the cities
of the rooms and classrooms and beds
he shall find fire in a fruit
always hanging there and odorous
for all of those seeking the earth
to hold and prolong.
Feeling therefore that his soul
was inhabited only by the presence
of those who never knew
the fresh buzz of the rivers
or the breeze
when it echoes in spaces
of continuity of the primordial juice
taking the seeds and offering them to the sun.
His soul is sad
and so is his blood
in which the urgency to harvest crams up
even in the desert-like venom.
The world's phrases don't speak to him
nor do words shine

with its harvest of unending depth.
Its foreign pupils have marched away
toward the horizon.
Immobile he discovers memory.
He sees how the linked cells of inertia
still inhabits the past of the primitive river
with the thunder and the great algae of dawn.
Toward the place he contemplates
he only finds
shining torsos escaping
hollow lips irremediably gnawing away
spasms agonizing with contagion
being left only with the sign of its own sight
toward earth
woman
child
old man
an injuring ditch
deep
so deep it is linked
to the countless weight of immensity.

Lightning from the Stable

Spanish

You don't choose
the abyss, the chaos, the nothingness
They reach you
in water running slowly
for you not to be surprised
by the absence of matter around you
near the light of the soul calling
the wing's passing flap of the earth you live in.

Alfonsina Storni

SWITZERLAND, 1892–1938

Squares and Angles

Spanish

Lined houses, lines houses,
lined houses.
Squares, squares, squares.
Lines houses.
People already have a squared soul,
lined ideas
and their back in an angle.
Yesterday I myself spilled a tear:
my God, it was square.

Very Little Man

Spanish

Very little man, very little man,
let your canary free since it wants to fly . . .
I am the canary, very little man,
let me out.

I was in a cage, very little man,
what a cage you have given me, very little man.
I say very little because you don't get what I say,
nor will you understand.

I don't understand you either, but meanwhile,
open the cage for me, for I want to escape;
very little man, I loved you for half a wing;
don't ask for more.

José Antonio Ramos Sucre VENEZUELA, 1890–1930

Prelude Spanish

I long to be in empty darkness, because the world cruelly injures my senses and life upsets me, impertinent lover conveying sorrows to me.

By then memories will have abandoned me: now they run away and return with the rhythm of tireless waves and are howling wolves in the night that covers the desert with snow.

Movement, bothering sign of reality, respects my astonishing asylum; but I will have climbed it arm in arm with death. She is a white Beatriz, and, standing on the crescent moon, shall visit the sea of my pains. Under its spell I shall rest forever and will no longer cry for the offended beauty or the impossible love.

Guillermo Sucre

VENEZUELA, 1933–

I Write with Words That Have Shadow but Don't Shelter

Spanish

I write with words that have shadow but don't shelter
no sooner do I start this page insomnia burns it
not the words but what they consume is what reality starts occupying
the place without place
the agony the game the illusion of being in the world

illusion is not what reality is made of but the ignited lightning
simulacra where ceremonies take place
bright exchanges from the emptiness of desire

there is no longer place for writing because writing is the place itself
of what is erased
we don't discover the world we describe it in its stubborn elusiveness

I shall no longer return to the sea but the sea lives in that absence
it is the sea when the word announces it
and is spilled over the page like a hand
I shall no longer be at the forest but in the page I write on
and I glimpse its foliage the wind passes by
there shall be no more summer but sun devouring memory
and the great night of sand coming to cover the eyes
and we shall only be able to read what wasn't written

Avrum Sutzkever

BELARUS, 1913–2010

Under Your White Stars

Yiddish

Under Your white stars
stretch to me Your white hand.
My words are tears,
wanting rest in Your hand.
Their spark dims
through my penetrating cellar eyes,
and I don't have a corner
to return them to You.
Yet I want, dear God,
to confide in You all I have,
for in me rages a fire
and in the fire, my days.
In cellars and holes
the murderous quiet weeps.
I run higher, even higher
and I search. Where are You, where?
Something strange pursues me
with lament across stairs and yards.
I hang a ruptured string,
and I sing to You:
Under Your white stars
stretch to me Your white hand.
My words are tears,
wanting rest in Your hand.

Jorge Teiller

CHILE, 1935–1996

A Poet of the Countryside

Spanish

after a Marc Chagall painting

Yes
we could also be lying down
prominently in the painting
with the raincoat covered with grass
and from our dream
perhaps
an indifferent horse would emerge
a slow-chewing cow
a helmet with a hay roof.

But
the point is
that things ought to dream with us,
and at the end no one ought to know
if it is us who are dreaming with the poet
that dreams this landscape
or it is the landscape that dreams with us
and the poet
and the painter.

Ana Enriqueta Terán

VENEZUELA, 1918–2017

Stone of Speech

Spanish

The poetess fulfills the measure and risk of the stone of speech.
Behaves as if through other ages and other struggles.
Sounds out the day only to discover the night in its autumn plumage.
Storms into the room of congregations dressed in the simplest act.
Kneels down with her wealth on the iguana's den . . .

Once everything is in place she returns to the place of origin. Place of insults.
Her sacred birds are denied, her cave with dim light, manner and strangeness.
Cowardice and bizarre daring in front of age and her points of solid gold.
The poetess responds for each fire, for each chimera, frown, height
repeated in equal sadness, in equal struggle for more shadow
for a little more sweetness for the aging rank.

The poetess offers her eagles. Shines in her birds of deep cloud.
Becomes owner of seasons, the four bitches of and the good and bad weather.
Becomes owner of rubble and bare land selected deliberately.
Thrusts a guacamaya where she shall kneel down.
The poetess fulfills the measure and risk of the stone of speech.

Outrageous Proof

Spanish

Then, revelation or greed, it was among you
slightly she bowed under the weight of dark collars;
covered by memories and floral customs
according to the first and most beautiful homeland drawn from summer.

Then, contribution or achieved dream, she wandered through you
strange and syllabic like a unique tree
adverted and coincidental in matters of satiety,
except God, the deprivation of God: ancient thirst,
eternal circumstance accompanied by the simplicity of heavenly bodies.

Then you were frightened by her gorgeous gray hares,
her closeness of stones that feels most,
her analysis of major beast, cosmic,

her innocence of woman combing her hair
making background music at the end of her hair.

Then you allowed her to leave
forgetting her intolerable verbal extension
and pallid Monday. Oh, daily Monday:
house, food and clean clothes for the men
the innumerable who builds his own God
with his immobile, crucified shadow
over rusty stations.

Nevertheless, it is she who restores your semblances,
counts your days
and shall return to her principles of radiant tree dated in the night.

César Vallejo

PERU, 1892–1938

Mass

Spanish

At the end of the battle,
and the fighter dead, a man came toward him
and said: "Don't die, I love you so much!"
But the corpse, ay!, went on dying.

Two came toward him and repeated:
"Don't leave us! Valor! Return to life!"
But the corpse, ay!, went on dying.

Twenty came to him, a hundred, a thousand, five-hundred-thousand,
clamoring: "So much love, and one is powerless before death!"
But the corpse, ay!, went on dying.

Millions of individuals surrounded him,
with a common plea: "Stay on, brother!"
But the corpse, ay!, went on dying.

Then, all the men on earth
surrounded him; the corpse, sad, emotional, saw them;
it slowly rose up,
it embraced the first man; he began to walk . . .

Blanca Varela

PERU, 1926–2009

Curriculum Vitae

Spanish

let's say that you won the race
and the prize
was another race
that you didn't savor the wine of victory
but your own salt
that you never listened to hurrahs
but dog barks
and your shadow
your own shadow
was your only
and disloyal competitor

Raúl Zurita

CHILE, 1950–

Heaven Reject

Spanish

I leave tomorrow papá. Tell mamá so. I'll clean
the bicycle rust and take the old path left by the
drying river. No more books papá. I'll leave
very early so mama doesn't notice it. You tell
her later papá. I won't say goodbye to anyone.
I would have liked to leave some flowers for
Veli, but for a long time the only flowers to be
found around here are stones. Deep is the well
of time. Can you see those mountains in the
background? Their tops are covered and it might
rain. Can you imagine the sea concealing again
this stone pile papá? You aren't talking to me papá.

Spanish

These are the last minutes of the evening of Monday, September 10, 1973, and the parades started less than an hour ago. For a moment the columns seem to have stopped before the burnt sky; a second later, the burst of instructions and chants inundate the streets. Ahead of us, interminable, a carpet of dried stones of the Pacific spreads out until disappearing in the horizon. I know that someone has probably been controlling my features, that is, controlling my insomnia, a certain nervousness, a way of talking recognized in the crushed stones on the edges of a port, Valparaíso, followed by a university façade (and, stuck to it, the broken images defining a life: an engineering career, a bunch of students rotating their menacing sticks, the maddening whiteness of waves breaking against the stones); suddenly, I heard the wind sound sweeping away the infinite drought of the soil. Did all this happened just a few seconds ago? Millions of years? A day? I raise my eyes. Motionless, the immense red sky floats over the multitude that also stops and now looks cold, fearful, as if in a dream, at the hopeless dusk.

1973

Spanish

They have bombed La Moneda and the stampede has taken shape. The streets are empty and at this time embassies are packed with people. I was taken prisoner in Valparaíso at dawn, but that doesn't matter. It matters that I need love and I'm alone. It doesn't matter either that the guys have escaped like rats. Such is life. I know a lot about it. Or at least I think so. It has left me behind a bit; I'm talking about life, of course. I had children and the woman who at that point was my first wife was searching for me. We had broken up a few months earlier, but still she was searching for me. I think truth is always something very simple. The guys ran to get lost and that's all. I would have done the same. I was taken into the cellar of a cargo ship. Bad stuff. I imagine her perfectly with my photo as a desaparecido hanging on her vest and she bothering people. I'm talking about the woman who was my wife, of course. A wonderful person, but I can imagine her perfectly. They escaped like rats. That's what I said. When I was first pushed around. I've started to type this because I'm alone and need a bit of love. The holes made by bombs have stayed there for many years. Whoever passes nearby does so quickly. No one stays around.

1974

Spanish

Those years were hard. The guys were everywhere,
loaded to their teeth, and they would mow you down
without fail and poor you. It was easy for them
to liquidate you once and for all. You could have
even thanked them for that. A German couple that had
just landed showed me the photos. It was the year
of the coup and it was an old story, but it was the first
time I saw them. The corpses had been swept away by
the Mapocho current. They popped up one morning
and people looked at them from the bridges. They
showed me the photos because a woman had made art
of them. She painted the corpses in the photograph in
flushed color and left the rest intact. Fuck the artists.
I went once to bed with that woman. It was in the
apartment where she and her partner lived, next to the
room where they slept, and the next day the three of
us had breakfast in the dinning-room. Before us, a big
window opened up to the interminable green of a golf
course. Truth is, everything was shit. Years after, we
crossed paths again. It was her father's funeral and
she seemed to me like a frightened girl. It's nothing
but a stupid dream, I told myself, but I called her
anyhow. Nicanor himself answered, perfectly alive,
and he sounded fine. When I left, it was almost noon
and I walked for hours without goal. The bodies
were painted with a pink wax pencil and looked like
small broken flowers amidst the gray of the
photograph. The river ran at their side. As if in a dream.

1980

Spanish

The woman showed me the photos while I jerked it
at an art gallery and things ended up bad. In the end,
all this masturbation about art under tyranny is blah
blah blah. With that woman, and with the woman
who became my second wife and with two more, I belonged
to a group of art activists under tyranny and blah
blah blah. There is another photograph. In it I'm
with the woman who was my wife at the beach and
it belongs to the same period. I'm sitting and she's
lying down on her side, wearing a black dress with
long sleeves. A few weeks earlier, the woman with
whom I jerked my self off had told me the other woman
was on the telephone. She knows you're here, she
said. I stood up and left. I delayed coming back
while thinking what to say so I returned after the
curfew. She had locked herself up in her room and
I didn't see her until the next day. It was carnage.
She had cut herself from head to toe with a
Gillette and burnt her legs and arms with the iron.
Some long, white tongues could be seen through
the black lines of her dress. It was windy on the
beach and in the photo one can see a portion of sea.
Her long sleeves covered the bandages on her arms
and the dress swirled around hiding her injured legs.
Later on, I had to live up to it really bad. There was
no way back. In any case: little broken people in a
little broken country. But in the photograph she had a
serene expression, peaceful, as if we had been happy.

Appendix Otra Vez and Más o Menos

Emily Dickinson UNITED STATES OF AMERICA, 1830–1886

Poema 239 English

"Paraíso" es lo que no alcanzo!
Manzana que en el Árbol vi –
Mientras siga en vano – cuelgue
Eso – "Paraíso" es – a Mí.

El color, en la Nube Pasajera –
La Tierra prohibida –
Detrás de la Cuesta –la Casa escondida –
Allí – Paraíso – Hallado!

Sus Púrpuras burlonas – las Tardes –
Los creyentes – atraídos –
Enamorados – del Conjurador –
Que nos tejió – Ayer!

Poema 288 English

Yo soy Nadie! Tú eres quién?
Eres – Nadie – También?
Pues somos dos los dos!
No lo digas! lo anunciarán – ya sabes!

Qué odioso – ser – Alguien!
Cuán público – como una Rana –
Decir tu nombre – en todo Junio –
Al pantano que clama!

Poema 441 English

Esta es mi carta al Mundo
Que nunca Me escribió —
Las simples noticias que la Naturaleza dijo —
Con tierna Majestad

Su Mensaje está cifrado
En Manos que no puedo ver —
En el amor por Ella — Dulce — compatriotas —
Júzguenme tiernamente

Poema 917

English

Amor — es anterior a la Vida —
Posterior — a la Muerte —
Origen de la Creación, y
Exponente de la Tierra —

Poema 1017

English

Morir – sin Morirse
Y vivir – sin la Vida
Este es el Milagro a cuestas
Propuesto del Creer.

Poema 1354

English

El Corazón es la Capital de la Mente –
La Mente un solo Estado –
El Corazón a la Mente siempre conectado
Un solo Continente –

Una – es la Población –
Bastante numerosa –
Esta extática Nación –
Búscala – eres Tú.

Robert Frost

UNITED STATES OF AMERICA, 1874–1963

Muro que separa

English

Algo hay que no quiere un muro,
Que revuelve el subsuelo helado bajo él,
Y dispersa las altas rocas bajo el sol;
Y surca hoyos que hasta dos pasan de frente.
La labor de cazadores es otra cosa:
Yo los he seguido y hecho reparos
Donde han dejado ni una piedra encima de otra,
Pero han tenido la liebre sin escondite,
Para complacer a perros aullando. Los hoyos,
Digo, nadie los ha visto u oído hacer,
Pero en época de composturas en primavera
Los encontramos ahí. Le dejo saber a mi vecino
Más allá del monte; y en un día en que nos
Encontramos para seguir la línea y fijar
El muro entre nosotros nuevamente.
Mantenemos el muro entre nosotros al andar.
A cada cual las rocas que han caído a cada quien.
Y algunas tienen panes y otras casi bolas
Debemos usar un hechizo para balancearlas:
"¡Mantente donde estás hasta que demos la espalda!"
Nuestros dedos se encallan con el esfuerzo.
Ah, solo otro tipo de juego al aire libre,
Uno de cada lado. El esfuerzo es escaso:
Allí donde está no necesitamos un muro:
Él es puro pino y yo manzanar.
Mis árboles de manzana nunca cruzarán
A comer los conos bajo sus pinos, le digo.
Él solo dice, "A buena reja buen vecino".
La primavera es mi travesura, y me pregunto
Si pudiera plantar una noción en su mente:
"¿*Por qué* hacen buenos vecinos? ¿No es
Donde hay vacas? Pero aquí no hay vacas.
Antes de levantar un muro quisiera saber
Lo que estoy amurallando adentro y afuera,

Y a quién acaso pueda yo ofender.
Hay algo que no quiere un muro,
Que lo quiere ausente". Podría decirle, "Elfos"
Pero no son elfos exactamente, y preferiría
Que él lo dijera por sí mismo. Lo veo allí
Cargando en alto una piedra en cada mano,
Como un salvaje antiguo armado.
Se mueve en la oscuridad me parece a mí,
No solo en bosques y la sobra de árboles.
No irá detrás del dictamen de su padre,
Y le gusta haberlo pensado tan bien,
Que dice otra vez: "A buena reja buen vecino".

Elizabeth Bishop

UNITED STATES OF AMERICA, 1911–1979

Un arte

English

El arte de extraviarse no es un misterio;
tantas cosas contienen en sí el accidente
de extraviarse, pero perderlas no es nada serio.

Extravía algo cada día. Acepta, confuso,
las llaves perdidas, la hora gastada inútilmente.
El arte de extraviar no es nada serio.

Después pierde más rápido, con criterio:
lugares, y nombres, y cuál era la escala subsecuente
de tu viaje. Nada de eso es serio.

Extravié el reloj de mi madre. ¡Y mira!, cedió
la penúltima de mis tres casas, o la siguiente.
El arte de extraviar no es nada serio.

Perdí dos ciudades, queridas ellas. Y el imperio
que era mío, dos ríos, un continente.
Los extraño, pero nada de eso es serio.

—Aun perderte a ti (la cariñosa voz, el gesto
que amo) no cambia nada. Es evidente
que el arte de extraviar no es un misterio
aunque parezca que es (¡*Escríbelo*!) muy serio.

Richard Wilbur

UNITED STATES OF AMERICA, 1921–2017

La prueba

English

¿Debo amar a Dios por permitir que fuera?
Yo, que mero verbo soy; ¿si amor su expresión me diera?

Porque al yo hacer que su obra tropezara,
Y un tema libre su gramática quebrara,

Lo amo porque hizo él desde su conmoción
Que en la página yo tuviera mi ocasión,

Y creyendo que quizás de mí un placer saldría,
Tachó *borrar* y un paciente *dejar* escribiría.

Walt Whitman

UNITED STATES OF AMERICA, 1819–1892

América

English to Spanglish

Centro de iguales daughters, iguales sons,
Todos, todos alike endear'd, grown, ungrown, jóvenes o viejos,
Fuertes, ample, fair, perdurables, capable, ricos,
Perenes con la Tierra, con la Libertad, la Ley y el Amor,
A grand, sane, towering, seated Madre,
Chair'd in the adamant del Tiempo.

William Shakespeare

ENGLAND, 1564–1616

Ser, or not to ser

English to Spanglish

Ser, or not to ser: esa es la question.
Whether 'tis nobler sufrir en la mente
The slings y flechas of outrageous fortuna,
O tomar las arms against un mar de troubles,
Y al oponerlos end them? Morir, dormir,
No more, y, by domir to say que terminamos
The heart-ache y los mil natural shoques
Que la carne is heir to—'tis a consumación
Devoutly to be deseada. Morir, dormir;
Dormir, perchance soñar: ay, there's el obstáculo:
For in that sueño of death what sueños may come
Cuando hemos shuffled off this coil mortal
Must darnos pausa. There's el respecto
That makes calamidad of una vida tan larga:
For quién puede soportar the whips and scorns del tiempo,
El opresor's wrong, the proud man's contumely,
Los pangs of dispriz'd amor, the law's retraso,
La insolencia of office, y los spurns
Que ameritan pacientemente the unworthy takes,
Cuando él mismo might his quietus make
Con a bare bodkin? who would fardels bear,
Gruñir y jurar under a weary vida,
But that the dread of algo después de la muerte,
The undiscover'd país de cuyo bourn
No viajero retorna, puzzles the will,
Y makes us rather bear esos males we have
Than fly a otros that we no conocemos?
Thus la conciencia does make cobardes de todos nosotros;
Y thus the native hue de la resolución
Is sicklied o'er con el pálido cast del pensamiento,
Y empresas de gran pith y moment
With este regard sus currents turn awry,
And lose el nombre de la acción. Soft you ahora!
The fair Ophelia! Nymph, in thy plegarias
Sean todos mis pecados remember'd.

Acknowledgements

Permission is gratefully acknowledged to the sources where these translations first appeared:

And We Came Out Again and Saw the Stars (2020): Andrés Neuman, "Genesis, COVID-19."

AGNI: Pablo Neruda, "Ode to Gratitude," "Ode to the Inconsequential Day," "Ode to Jean Arthur Rimbaud," and "Ode to the Names of Venezuela."

Asymptote: Yitzkhok Berliner, "Popocatépetl"; and Kayva Molodowsky, "God of Mercy."

The Common: Ferreira Gullar, "Translating Oneself," "Two Plus Two Is Four," and "Song to Avoid Death"; Besik Kharanauli, "We Should Dig Out Potatoes"; and Juan Carlos Marset, "Embraceable."

The FSG Book of Twentieth-Century Latin American Poetry (2011): Delmira Agustini, "*Fiera de amor*"; Humberto Ak'Abal, "The Dance" and "I Took Your Name Out of My Mind"; Alberto Blanco, "My Tribe" and "Maps"; Jorge Luis Borges, "Borges and I"; Julia de Burgos, "To Julia de Burgos"; Rubén Darío, "*Lo fatal*"; Juan Gelman, "End," "Dibaxu: I" and "Dibaxu: XII"; León de Grieff, "White Moon"; Vicente Huidobro, "Globe-Trotter"; Darío Jamarillo Agudelo, "Love Poem 8" and "Vengeance"; Dulce María Loynáz, "The Mirror," "Love Is . . . ," and "I Dream of Classifying . . ."; Leopoldo Lugones, "History of My Death"; Eugenio Montejo, "Earthliness" and "Ithaca": Álvaro Mutis, "Lament for the Death of Marcel Proust"; Gonzalo Rojas, "André Breton Turns a Hundred and Is Fine"; Alfonsina Storni, "Squares and Angles" and "Very Little Man"; Jorge Teiller, "A Poet of the Countryside"; César Vallejo, "Mass"; Blanca Varela, "Curriculum Vitae"; and Raúl Zurita, "Heaven Reject" and "These are the last moments."

Lengua Fresca (2012): Emily Dickinson, "Poema 239," "Poema 288," "Poema 917," "Poema 1017," and "Poema 1354"; and Richard Wilbur, "La prueba."

Lit Hub: José Hernández, "*The Gaucho Martín Fierro*, Part One, Canto 1, 1-19"; William Shakespeare, "Ser, o not to ser."

Los Angeles Review of Books: Carlos Drummond de Andrade, "International Congress of Fear"; and Federico García Lorca, "At a Young Woman's Ear" and "Ode to Walt Whitman."

Massachusetts Review: Raúl Zurita, "1973," "1974," and "1980."

New York Times: Juan Gelman, "Epitaph."

The Norton Anthology of Latino Literature (2011): José Martí, "Two Homelands."

Pablo Neruda: All the Odes (2014): "Ode to Air," "Ode to the Andean Cordillera," "Ode to Ángel Cruchaga," "Ode to the Apple," "Ode to the Flowers of Datitla," "Ode to the Dictionary," "Ode to Guatemala," "Ode to the Month of August," "Ode to the Moon," "Ode to the Murmur," "Ode to Night," "Ode to Simplicity," "Ode to Things," and "Ode to the Watermelon."

Pablo Neruda: I Explain a Few Things (2007): "The Son" and "Your Laughter."

El País: Emily Dickinson, "Poema 441"; Robert Frost, "Muro que separa"; Elizabeth Bishop, "Un arte"; and Walt Whitman, "America."

Pakhn Treger: Kadya Molodowsky, "God of Mercy"; and Avrum Sutzkever, "Under Your White Stars."

Paper Brigade: Yehuda Amichai, "The Diameter of the Bomb"; and Yehuda Halevi, "My Heart is in the East."

Sor Juana; or, The Persistence of Pop (2019): "Misguided Men"; and "Stay, Shadow."

Tablet: Jacqueline Goldberg, "Poetics"; and Ida Gramcko, "Jewish Cemetery (Prague) (fragment)" and "Snail, Brother."

World Literature Today: Guillermo Sucre, "I Write with Words That Have Shadow but Don't Shelter"; and Óscar Hahn, "Nude Descending a Staircase" and "In the Region of Water and Fire."

Index of Languages

ENGLISH

Elizabeth Bishop: "Un arte," 177

Emily Dickinson: "Poema 239," 173; "Poema 288," 173; "Poema 441," 173; "Poema 917," 174; "Poema 1017," 174; "Poema 1354," 174

Robert Frost: "Muro que separa," 175

Richard Wilbur: "La prueba," 178

Walt Whitman: "América," 179

William Shakespeare: "Ser, or not to ser," 180

FRENCH

Vicente Huidobro: "Globe-Trotter," 49

GEORGIAN

Besik Kharanauli: "We Should Dig Out Potatoes," 57

GERMAN

Paul Celan: "Death Fugue," 21

HEBREW

Yehuda Amichai: "The Diameter of the Bomb," 7

Yehuda Halevi: "My Heart Is in the East," 46

K'ICHE'

Humberto Ak'Abal: "The Dance," 4

LADINO

Juan Gelman: "Dibaxu: I," 35; "Dibaxu: XII," 36

PORTUGUESE

Carlos Drummond de Andrade: "International Congress of Fear," 26
Ferreira Gullar: "Translating Oneself," 41; "Two Plus Two Is Four," 42; "Song to Avoid Death," 43
João Pinto Delgado: "Leaving Egypt," 151

RUSSIAN

Anna Akhmatova: "The Muse," 6

SPANGLISH

Walt Whitman: "América," 179
William Shakespeare: "Ser, or not to ser," 180

SPANISH

Delmira Agustini: "*Fiera de amor*," 3
Humberto Ak'Abal: "I Took Your Name Out of My Mind," 5
Enriqueta Arévalo Larriva: "We Were Not the Whole Tree," 8
Alberto Blanco: "My Tribe," 11; "Maps," 13
Jorge Luis Borges: "Borges and I," 17
Julia de Burgos: "To Julia de Burgos," 18
María Calcaño: "Cosmos," 20
Luis Alberto Crespo: "Hurts," 23
Rubén Darío: "*Lo fatal*," 25
Federico García Lorca: "At a Young Woman's Ear," 27; "Ode to Walt Whitman," 28
Juan Gelman: "End," 33; "Epitaph," 34
Jacqueline Goldberg: "Poetics," 37
Ida Gramcko: "Jewish Cemetery (Prague) (fragment)," 38; "Snail, Brother," 39
León de Grieff: "White Moon," 40
Óscar Hahn: "Nude Descending a Staircase," 44; "In the Region of Water and Fire," 45
José Hernández: "*The Gaucho Martín Fierro*, Part One, Canto I, 1–19," 47
Sor Juana Inés de La Cruz: "Misguided Men," 51; "Stay, Shadow," 54
Darío Jamarillo Agudelo: "Love Poem 8," 55; "Vengeance," 56
Juan Liscano: "Body of Love," 64
Dulce María Loynáz: "The Mirror," 65; "Love Is . . . ," 67; "I Dream of Classifying . . . ," 68

Leopoldo Lugones: "History of My Death," 69
Juan Carlos Marset: "Embraceable," 70
José Martí: "Two Homelands," 71
Eugenio Montejo: "Earthliness," 74; "Ithaca," 75
Álvaro Mutis: "Lament for the Death of Marcel Proust," 77
Pablo Neruda: "Your Laughter," 79; "The Son," 81; "Ode to Age," 83; "Ode to the Andean Cordillera," 85; "Ode to Ángel Cruchaga," 89; "Ode to the Apple," 92; "Ode to the Flowers of Datitla," 94; "Ode to the Dictionary," 98; "Ode to Gratitude," 101; "Ode to Guatemala," 103; "Ode to the Inconsequential Day," 110; "Ode to Jean Arthur Rimbaud," 113; "Ode to the Month of August," 118; "Ode to the Moon," 121; "Ode to the Murmur," 126; "Ode to the Names of Venezuela," 130; "Ode to Night," 133; "Ode to Simplicity," 136; "Ode to Things," 140; "Ode to the Watermelon," 144
Andrés Neuman: "Genesis, COVID-19," 147
Antonia Palacios: "That Obscure Animal of Dream," 149; "Writings of Eviction," 150
Gonzalo Rojas: "André Breton Turns a Hundred and Is Fine," 152
Elizabeth Schön: "From the Ancient Laborer I," 153; "Lightning from the Stable," 155
Alfonsina Storni: "Squares and Angles," 156; "Very Little Man," 157
José Antonio Ramos Sucre: "Prelude," 158
Guillermo Sucre: "I Write with Words that Have Shadow but Don't Shelter," 159
Jorge Teiller: "A Poet of the Countryside," 161
Ana Enriqueta Terán: "Stone of Speech," 162; "Outrageous Proof," 163
César Vallejo: "Mass," 164
Blanca Varela: "Curriculum Vitae," 165
Raúl Zurita: "Heaven Reject," 166; "These are the last moments," 167; "1973," 168; "1974," 169; "1980," 170

YIDDISH

Yitzkhok Berliner: "Popocatépetl," 9
Kadya Molodowsky: "God of Mercy," 72
Avrum Sutzkever: "Under Your White Stars," 160

Index of Titles and First Lines

A bird lived in me., 34
A grand nakedness, 20
A part of me, 41
Ah son, do you know, do you know, 81
Algo hay que no quiere un muro, 175
All of us dance, 4
Along the East River and the Bronx, 28
Already people murmur I'm your enemy, 18
"América" (Whitman), 179
Amor — es anterior a la Vida —, 174
And the Pope said amen in the empty square, 147
"André Breton Turns a Hundred and Is Fine" (Rojas), 152
Ángel, I remember, 89
"arte, Un" (Bishop), 177
"At a Young Woman's Ear" (García Lorca), 27
At night, as I await her arrival, 6
At the end of the battle, 164

Back like an ox, beast, 94
Beast of love, I suffer hunger for hearts., 3
Behind, 133
Bird without leaves, 24
Black milk in the morning we drink you at dawn, 21
"Body of Love" (Liscano), 64
"Borges and I" (Borges), 17

Centro de iguales daughters, iguales sons, 179
Clock of the sky, 121
"Cosmos" (Calcaño), 20
"Curriculum Vitae" (Varela), 165

"Dance, The" (Ak'Abal), 4
"Death Fugue" (Celan), 21
¿Debo amar a Dios por permitir que fuera?, 178
"Diameter of the Bomb, The" (Amichai), 7
"Dibaxu: I" (Gelman), 35
"Dibaxu: XII" (Gelman), 36

"Earthliness" (Montejo), 74
El arte de extraviarse no es un misterio;, 177
El Corazón es la Capital de la Mente –, 174
"Embraceable" (Marset), 70
"End" (Gelman), 33
Esta es mi carta al Mundo, 173
"Epitaph" (Gelman), 34

"*Fiera de amor*" (Agustini), 3
Flames swimming in living water, 45
"From the Ancient Laborer I" (Schön), 153

"*Gaucho Martin Fierro, The*, Part One, Canto 1, 1–19" (Hernández), 47
"Genesis, COVID-19" (Neuman), 147
"Globe-Trotter" (Huidobro), 49
Gracias to the word, 101
"God of Mercy" (Molodowsky), 72
God of Mercy, 72
Guatemala, 103

"Heaven Reject" (Zurita), 166
Herein the suit, 44
"History of My Death" (Lugones), 69
"Hurts" (Crespo), 23

I am dying. I am dying a slow death, silent, without noise., 150
I didn't want to., 27
I don't believe in age., 83
"I Dream of Classifying . . ." (Loynáz), 68
I dreamed of classifying, 68
I dreamed of death and it was quite simple:, 69
I have two homelands: Cuba and the Night., 71
I leave tomorrow papá. Tell mamá so. I'll clean, 166
I long to be in empty darkness, 158

I love crazy things, 140
I once again return, 118
"Ithaca" (Montejo), 75
"I Took Your Name Out of My Mind" (Ak'Abal), 5
I took your name out of my mind, 5
"I Write with Words that Have Shadow but Don't Shelter" (Sucre), 159
I write with words that have shadow but don't shelter, 159
If appearance, mirage, if illusion of nothingness, 64
"In the Region of Water and Fire" (Hahn), 45
In this fierce Egypt, 151
In what corner of your alcove, before which mirror, 77
"International Congress of Fear" (Drummond de Andrade), 26
Irreplaceable you, 70

"Jewish Cemetery (Prague)" (fragment) (Gramcko), 38
Just as two and two is four, 42

"Lament for the Death of Marcel Proust" (Mutis), 77
"Leaving Egypt" (Pinto Delgado), 151
let's say that you won the race, 165
Let's start at the beginning:, 13
"Lightning from the Stable" (Schön), 155
Lined houses, lines houses, 156
"*Lo fatal*" (Darío), 25
"Love Is . . ." (Loynáz), 67
"Love Poem 8" (Jamarillo Agudelo), 55

Many are the doors, many the crevices, 149
"Maps" (Blanco), 13
"Mass" (Vallejo), 164
"Mirror, The" (Loynáz), 65
"Misguided Men" (de la Cruz), 51
Morir – sin Morirse, 174
"Muro que separa" (Frost), 175
"Muse, The" (Akhmatova), 6
"My Heart Is in the East" (Halevi), 46
My heart is in the east, and I am in the far-away west., 46
"My Tribe" (Blanco), 11

"1973" (Zurita), 168
"1974" (Zurita), 169

"1980" (Zurita), 170
Now, 113
Now you, turned into a poem, 56
"Nude Descending a Staircase" (Hahn), 44

"Obscure Animal of Dream, That" (Palacios), 149
"Ode to Age" (Neruda), 83
"Ode to the Andean Cordillera" (Neruda), 85
"Ode to Ángel Cruchaga" (Neruda), 89
"Ode to the Apple" (Neruda), 92
"Ode to the Dictionary" (Neruda), 94
"Ode to the Flowers of Datitla" (Neruda), 98
"Ode to Gratitude" (Neruda), 101
"Ode to Guatemala" (Neruda), 103
"Ode to the Inconsequential Day" (Neruda), 110
"Ode to Jean Arthur Rimbaud" (Neruda), 113
"Ode to the Month of August" (Neruda), 118
"Ode to the Moon" (Neruda), 121
"Ode to the Murmur" (Neruda), 126
"Ode to the Names of Venezuela" (Neruda), 130
"Ode to Night" (Neruda), 133
"Ode to Simplicity" (Neruda), 136
"Ode to Things" (Neruda), 140
"Ode to the Watermelon" (Neruda), 144
Once again, from up high, 85
Order suffers, what is racked with pain ends, 38
"Outrageous Proof" (Terán), 163

"Paraíso" es lo que no alcanzo!, 173
"Poema 239" (Dickinson), 173
"Poema 288" (Dickinson), 173
"Poema 441" (Dickinson), 173
"Poema 917" (Dickinson), 174
"Poema 1017" (Dickinson), 174
"Poema 1354" (Dickinson), 174
"Poet of the Countryside, A" (Teiller), 161
"Poetics" (Goldberg), 37
Popo—, 9
"Popocatépetl" (Berliner), 9
"Prelude" (Ramos Sucre), 158

Provisionally we shall not sing to love, 26
"prueba, La" (Wilbur), 178

"Ser, or not to ser" (Shakespeare), 180
Ser, or not to ser: esa es la question., 180
Silver fish, 110
Simplicity, I ask you:, 136
"Snail, Brother" (Gramcko), 39
Snail, brother, 39
"Son, The" (Neruda), 81
"Song to Avoid Death" (Gullar), 43
"Squares and Angles" (Storni), 156
"Stay, Shadow" (de la Cruz), 54
Stay, shadow, 54
"Stone of Speech" (Terán), 162
Stubborn men, who will chastise, 51
Suddenly the poet's mouth is overwhelmed by larvae, 37

Take bread away from me, if you wish, 79
The crack without house, 23
The diameter of the bomb was thirty centimeters, 7
The earth is the same, 11
The man dresses up, 153
The mirror hanging on the wall, 65
The other one, Borges, is to whom things happen., 17
The plains, once again burned, 130
The poetess fulfills measure and risk of the stone of speech., 162
The time Breton died we all got together, 152
The tree is happy for it is barely sentient, 25
the tremor on my lips/, 35
The woman showed me the photos while I jerked it, 170
Then, revelation or greed, it was among you, 163
"These are the last moments" (Zurita), 167
These are the last minutes of the evening of Monday, 167
They have bombed La Moneda and the stampede, 168
Those years were hard. The guys were everywhere, 169
Through this road one gets to Ithaca, 75
To be here on earth for years on end, 74
"To Julia de Burgos" (de Burgos), 18
To love the delicate grace, 67

"Translating Oneself" (Gullar), 41
Tree of summer, 144
"Two Homelands" (Martí), 71
"Two Plus Two Is Four" (Gullar), 42

Under the pines, the earth concocts, 98
"Under Your White Stars" (Sutzkever), 160
Under Your white stars, 160

"Vengeance" (Jamarillo Agudelo), 56
Verses of love, of mourning, 126
"Very Little Man" (Storni), 157
Very little man, very little man, 157
"We Were Not the Whole Tree" (Arévalo Larriva), 8
We were not the whole tree. Only graceful, 8
"We Should Dig Out Potatoes" (Kharanauli), 57
"We should dig out potatoes tomorrow!," 57
What I'm about to tell you is a rare tale, 47
what you gave me, 36
When you go away, 43
"White Moon" (de Grieff), 40
White moon . . . and cold . . . , 40
"Writings of Eviction" (Palacios), 150

Yes, 161
Yo soy Nadie! Tú eres quién?, 173
You, apple, 92
Your blue glance, 49
You don't choose, 155
"Your Laughter" (Neruda), 79
Your tongue, your wise tongue that invents my skin, 55